CULTURES OF THE WORLD

JAPAN

Rex Shelley

MARSHALL CAVENDISH
New York • London • Sydney

Editorial Director	Shirley Hew
Managing Editors	Mark Dartford
	Shova Loh
Editors	Goh Sui Noi
	Meena Mylvaganam
	Cheryl M. English
Picture Editor	Jane Duff
Production	Jeremy Chan
	Robert Paulley
	Julie Cairns
Design	Tuck Loong
	Doris Nga
	Stella Liu
	Lee Woon Hong
Illustrators	Francis Oak
	Vincent Chew
	Thomas Koh

Reference edition published 1991 by
Marshall Cavendish Corporation
2415 Jerusalem Avenue
North Bellmore
N.Y. 11710

Printed in Singapore

Originated and designed by
Times Books International
an imprint of Times Editions Pte Ltd
Times Center, 1 New Industrial Road
Singapore 1953
Telex: 37908 EDTIME Fax: 2854871

Library of Congress Cataloging-in-Publication Data:
Shelley, Rex, 1930–
      Japan/Rex Shelley.—Reference ed.
        p. cm.—(Cultures of the world)
      Includes bibliographical references.
      Summary: Introduces the geography,
history, religious beliefs, government, and people
of Japan.
      ISBN 1-85435-297-0: $19.95
      1. Japan [1. Japan.] I. Title.
II. Series.
DS806.S45 1990
952—dc20   89–23877
                                     CIP
                                     AC

INTRODUCTION

IT HAS BEEN SAID that Japan is a nation of the 21st century. This is because it is a highly industrialized nation whose corporate giants are legend; names such as Sony, Mitsubishi, Seiko, Panasonic, Honda and Sanyo are household words. The Japanese devote much energy to competing with each other and with the rest of the world, for to be first and to attain only the best means a great deal to them.

Yet Japan is a nation of romantic traditions. The Japanese seek spiritual inspiration through nature, as well as through their association with temples and shrines. Japanese literature and art give many clues to their deep involvement with legends.

Do we know enough about this important country and its people?

Through their history, lifestyle, festivals and many other aspects, this book goes beyond mere statistics to help us understand the Japanese. It is one of the series, *Cultures of the World*—a look at people and their lifestyles.

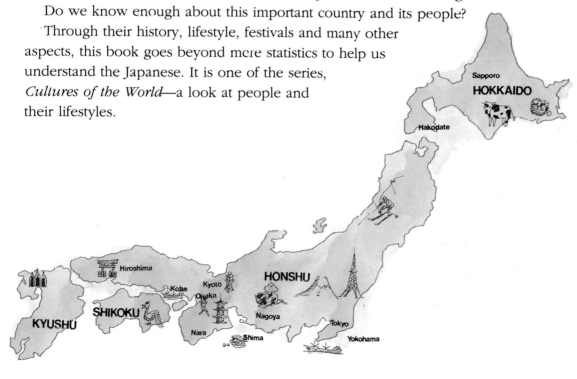

CONTENTS

The bell-rope is pulled before prayers in a Shinto shrine.

CONTENTS

Tokyo Tower, both a broadcasting and sight-seeing tower, is a replica of the French Eiffel Tower in Paris.

GEOGRAPHY

JAPAN LIES on longitude 139°46' East. To the Europeans, Japan is "the Far East." The word "Japan" is derived from the Japanese "Nippon," meaning "sun's origin," because the Japanese believed that the sun first shone on Japan. The country is also known as the Land of the Rising Sun.

Japan consists of four thousand mountainous islands, in a bow-shaped cluster. The four largest islands form the core of Japan, and of these, Honshu, the central and largest island, is the living heart. In the past, Imperial and feudal powers were concentrated on Honshu. Today, the island is the industrial hub of modern Japan and home to 80% of the population. The highest mountain (Mt. Fuji, 12,389 feet), the longest river (Shinano, 228 miles) and the largest lake (Biwa) are on Honshu.

South of Honshu is Shikoku, the smallest of the four major islands. Although so close to Honshu, Shikoku has been a rustic appendage to the mainstream of activity and development. At the southern end of Honshu lies the island of Kyushu. It has a subtropical climate and, in a way, is the "sunshine state" of Japan. It is the island nearest to Korea and to the cultural influences of China.

To the north lies the large island, Hokkaido. It is the Alaska of Japan, with bitter cold winters and harsh volcanic mountains. It was once an island for outcasts.

Opposite: **The Deer Park at Nara in Honshu. In the distance, a very common sight, a religious shrine.**

Right: **Symmetrical and serene, Mt. Fuji.**

Opposite top: **In 1986 Mt. Miharayama on Oshima, one of Japan's newer islands, erupted violently, and molten lava threatened to engulf its main city.**

"In 1910 Mount Usu erupted with such violence that a new mountain was formed in the convulsions. In 1944 it erupted again and a second new mountain grew up beside the first. To the Japanese people ... the island (Hokkaido) must resemble a half-wild animal."

— Allan Booth,
Roads to Sata

A LAND OF MOUNTAINS

Japan was once part of the great Asian continent. Sometime in the Ice Age, the islands were separated from the Asian land mass and the peaks of the old continent became the four thousand islands of Japan. The average elevation of the four main islands is 1,000 feet. The Pacific Ocean to the east and south and the Sea of Japan between Japan and China did not erode the land and change it significantly. Neither did the volcanoes, although Japan lies at the confluence of two volcanic belts that ring a large part of the Pacific. There are about 67 "live" volcanoes, that is, volcanoes that are either active or potentially active. Mt. Fuji, Japan's highest mountain, is a volcano. The Japanese call it "Fujiyama-san" (*yama* means "mountain" and *san* is a complimentary form of "Mister"). This mountain is their spiritual symbol.

About 72% of Japan is mountainous and too steep for development. These steep slopes sent the Japanese down to the sea, to ships and fishing. Every major city is located on the edge of the sea.

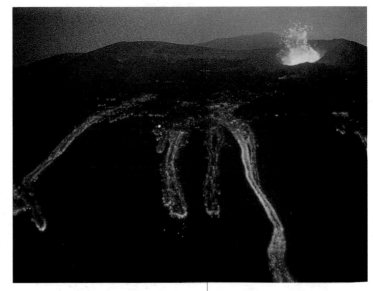

As island people do everywhere, the Japanese turned to the sea for their sustenance and dreams. The mountains are, however, always in the background, helping to shape the Japanese character, teaching stoic resilience. Because of volcanic eruptions, the Japanese had to fashion their buildings to meet upheavals. Using the products of mountain forests, they built timber and paper houses which kept them cool in hot summers but could not insulate them against the harsh winter cold. The paper houses are almost all gone now.

EARTHQUAKES

On September 1, 1923 the greatest earthquake in Japan's history shook the western part of Honshu around and to the north of Tokyo. The death toll from the earthquake and the ensuing fires was about 100,000. The old Tokyo, known as Edo, was flattened, but within four years modern Tokyo had risen from the ruins.

Earthquakes are a constant danger in Japan. If they occur near the surface, the damage can be tremendous. If they occur along the ocean floor, they generate *tsunami*, 60–100 foot-high tidal waves capable of wiping out entire coastal areas.

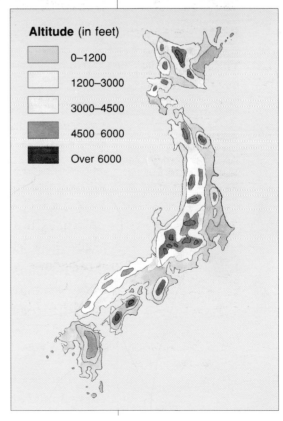

Altitude (in feet)

0–1200

1200–3000

3000–4500

4500 6000

Over 6000

RIVERS AND LAKES

The rain- and snow-fed rivers of Japan are small and swift, many of them hurtling like waterfalls to the sea. There are numerous lakes. Lakes have always held a great fascination for the Japanese. It is probably the calm of a lake as an inland sea that attracts these island and mountain people spiritually: calm, still water appearing unexpectedly in the ruggedness of the mountains. Lake Biwa, located on Honshu, is Japan's largest and most beautiful lake. It is revered by the Japanese for its historical and cultural significance.

CLIMATE

If it were not for three major factors, Japan, as an island-nation, would enjoy a mild and pleasant temperate climate. These factors are the large air mass over Siberia; the warm, moist air blowing in from the Pacific; and, cutting across these air currents, the mountain ranges that run perpendicular to the direction of the winds.

During the winter months, December to February, Siberia's high-pressure areas cause periodic cold waves to flow south, lowering the temperature throughout Japan. As the winds from central Siberia cross the Sea of Japan, they meet warm air currents flowing northward, absorb large amounts of moisture, and deposit it as snow in the mountains. As a result, Japan has one of the heaviest snowfalls in the world.

During the summer months, June to August, Japan comes under the influence of the high pressure areas of the Pacific and the low pressures over Siberia. The airstreams flow north and east, bringing heat and moisture. Tokyo and Osaka, in particular, are unbearably hot and humid at this time. The highest temperature ever recorded in Tokyo is 102° Fahrenheit.

The winds change in spring and fall, the most pleasant times in Japan.

PLUM RAINS AND TYPHOONS In early summer, cold currents of air flowing from the north meet moist currents from the South Pacific and there are periods of rainy weather. Rains can be intense at times, causing floods and crop damage, but these early summer rains make it possible to grow rice in Japan. The Japanese call them Plum Rains and write poetry about them.

At the end of summer, Japan is subjected to the typhoons blowing in from the Pacific. These winds produced in subtropical areas can reach a speed of 130 miles an hour at the center (the "eye" of the storm). Like cyclones and hurricanes, typhoons cause great damage; but they also bring rain.

VEGETATION

Japan's climate, ranging from subtropical to temperate and cold, encourages the growth of a great variety of trees. Mangrove swamps are found in the coastal region of the southern Ryukyus, while in Kyushu, Shikoku and southern Honshu, evergreens flourish. Mountain forests in central and northern Honshu are rich with broadleaf deciduous trees such as maple, ash, birch, beech and poplar. Evergreens there include fir, spruce, larch, hemlock and Japanese cedar. Pines and the white beech grow in Hokkaido. From spring to fall, Japanese forests are a spectacular sight.

RANDOM FACTS ABOUT JAPAN'S ANIMAL LIFE

Native primate*:* Japanese macaque.

Largest snake*:* Japanese rat snake, 5 feet long and harmless.

Famous amphibian*:* A species of giant salamander, one of the largest living amphibians, reaching 5 feet in length, lives in Kyushu and western Honshu.

Notorious insect*:* The Japanese beetle, accidentally imported into the Americas in 1916. A swarm of Japanese beetles can denude a peach tree in 15 minutes, leaving only branches and pits.

Japanese beetle.

HISTORY

BEGINNINGS

JAPANESE HISTORY starts at about the time of Christ. Scholars differ about events before this as there is limited data. The only sources of information are two chronicles written in the 8th century, the *Kojiki* (*Records of Ancient Matters*, A.D. 712) and the *Nihongi* (*Written Chronicles of Japan*, A.D. 720). Both describe an elaborate mythology.

The early Japanese, a Mongoloid race, were migrants from China, Korea and Manchuria who came across the Tsushima straits to southwestern Honshu (some believe at Izuma) and Kyushu. Scholars have suggested that migrants may also have included people of Malay stock from Oceania, the islands of the Pacific.

The early settlers found a strange and uncivilized aboriginal people, the Ainu, a Neolithic people who looked more Caucasian than Mongoloid, with hairy skin and round eyes. The migrants from the Asian continent slowly penetrated the whole country, pushing the Ainu northward.

Opposite: **A *haniwa* of a priestess. Archeologists think that these clay sculptures were buried with rich or famous people, in place of human sacrifice.**

THE FIRST JAPANESE EMPEROR

Japan's early history was marked by contact with China. It was a time riddled with struggles for power and territory. In the 7th century, one strong man emerged: Jimmu Tenno, leader of the Yamato clan and first emperor of the Imperial line.

In mythology, Japanese emperors are descendants of the sun goddess. The first emperor was given three sacred treasures: a bronze mirror, a sword and a bead (in another version, this is a string of precious stones). With these three treasures, he convinced the warring clans of his divine descent. His empire became a powerful one, centered in Nara. Only the melted bronze mirror remains, at the Imperial Shrine of Ise (see page 63).

Sculpture was refined in the Heian period, and reached its peak in the Kamakura period. On the right is an example of Heian sculpture housed in the Todaiji temple in Nara.

Opposite top: **A** *daimyo* (feudal chieftain) never travels without his *samurai.*

Opposite bottom: Takauji Ashikaga, a member of the Ashikaga family, who was appointed *Sei-I-Taishogun*, or barbarian-quelling general, in 1338.

HEIAN, A GOLDEN AGE

Japan enjoyed relative peace from A.D. 794 to 1185. The capital was moved from Nara to Heian-kyo, "capital of peace and calm," hence the "Heian period." Heian-kyo was later called Kyoto, simply "capital." The Japanese *kana* scripts were created and the arts flourished. The classic *Tale of the Genji* was written by Murasaki Shikibu (A.D. 1000), revealing many details of court life.

SHOGUN AND SAMURAI

While culture flourished, poverty of the masses provoked uprisings. Out of the skirmishes and battles to suppress these rebellions, Yoritomo Minamoto emerged as the most powerful warrior. He challenged the Emperor's authority and the ultimate power passed from the Imperial court and its aristocracy in Kyoto to the military supremo, the *Shogun.*

Yoritomo Minamoto established his seat of government at Kamakura in 1185. In 1192 he was conferred the title of *Shogun*.

It was during the period of the Kamakura shogunate (a dynasty of *Shogun*) that the ethical code of the *samurai* or Japanese warrior was developed. Japan was then a feudal society and the *samurai* were the armed champions of the leading families. They were called *gokenin*, "men of the family," and they gave unconditional loyalty.

ASHIKAGA SHOGUNATE In 1333, the Kamakura shogunate fell and the Ashikaga family took over. Their regime, which lasted until 1574, was wracked with rivalry and other troubles. The mountainous terrain made central control difficult and the country was split into warring states. However, regional sufficiency became important and there was considerable development of industries, transportation and public works.

A portrait of Ieyasu Tokugawa.

UNIFICATION UNDER THREE GREAT MEN

The 16th century was a time of major events in Japan's history. It also saw the rise of three great men: Nobunaga Oda, Hideyoshi Toyotomi and Ieyasu Tokugawa. These men unified the country and set the stage for the dawning of modern Japan.

Nobunaga Oda (1534–82) overpowered his rivals by the use of crude muskets that were being made in central Japan. In 1578 he was the leading figure who set himself the task of uniting Japan under the control of a single powerful authority. He succeeded in about half the country around Kyoto.

Hideyoshi Toyotomi (1536–98), one of Nobunaga Oda's generals, succeeded him. He was a small and ugly man, almost a dwarf, yet powerful and dynamic with a certain charm. His leadership was marked by the development of several institutions, including a new system of taxation to fund his invasion of Korea (which failed), and the growth of merchant centers. Japan enjoyed prosperity and stability under Toyotomi.

Ieyasu Tokugawa (1542–1616), who followed Toyotomi, established his position at the battle of Sekigahara in 1600. By 1603 he had been given the title of *Shogun*. This cool, unshakeable man of iron spent 40 years fighting, and developed into a high-caliber military commander as well as a faultless judge of character.

WESTERN INFLUENCE

The success of the three military strategists, Nobunaga Oda, Hideyoshi Toyotomi and Ieyasu Tokugawa, has to be seen against the background of western influence. In the middle of the 16th century, the first ships from the west arrived in Japan, bristling with Christian missionaries who made quite amazing progress with their conversions. They also brought the smooth bore musket that changed the strategies of feudal battles.

With this flow of Portuguese and Dutch into southern Japan came a most unusual Englishman, Will Adams. Adams worked his way up through the corridors of power to become a trusted adviser to the *Shogun*, Ieyasu Tokugawa. He later betrayed the trust placed in him by working with the Portuguese and Spanish against the Japanese.

The Christians brought with them many problems, not the least of which was the rivalry between the different Christian groups. They also stirred up new loyalties among the Japanese converts. The conflicts finally erupted in a siege of Shimabara in Kyushu (1638). No help arrived for the insurgents and they were all killed.

The *daimyo* (feudal chieftains) were kept constantly on the move to prevent them from consolidating power in their own territory. They were obliged to leave families permanently in Edo (old Tokyo), the seat of power. They were themselves required to live alternate years in their own territories and in Edo. Above is an artist's rendition of a typical *daimyo* procession to Edo. The route and the number of attendants were fixed by the *Shogun*.

ISOLATION AND THE SECOND INVASION

Below: **Arrival of Commodore Perry in Edo (old Tokyo).**

Opposite top: **German doctor, Erwin Bälz, one of many foreign advisers, lectured in Tokyo Imperial University for 26 years. He and another German, Julius Scriba, are known as "Fathers of Japanese Medicine."**

Opposite bottom: **An early Japanese mission (1871) sent overseas to study the conditions and customs in the west.**

The Tokugawa shogunate threw out all foreigners and closed the country to the world in 1637. No Japanese were allowed to travel out of Japan and there was even a restriction on the size of boat that could be constructed to make this edict effective. For the next two hundred years Japan was isolated from the world.

The Europeans, and the American pioneers who were building their colonial empires, however, had other ideas. In Russia, groups of financiers and traders with their eye on the profits Japan could yield managed to persuade their reluctant government to send a fleet to Japan. Admiral Putyatin arrived in Nagasaki in August 1853, hoping to force open the closed doors. He was preceded by an American, Commodore Perry, who had sailed into Tokyo in July with four vessels, two of them powered by steam. The Americans needed bases for their China trade; in particular, they needed coal for their steamships.

This was the second "invasion" of Japan by the west. The first had been in the guise of Christian missionary zeal four hundred years earlier.

The Japanese rulers were startled and shaken by the American demands. At the same time, from reports that trickled in through the Dutch, they realized that they were defenseless against the new military technology of the west. Taking a painful but realistic decision, they opened the door a crack.

TRANSFORMATION

The country swung into a period of learning and selective absorption of all things western, with a determination that is still unparalleled in human history. Within 50 years, Japan moved through hundreds of years of human thought and development, from feudalism to a modern nation.

They examined and sifted the new concepts and technologies, not through the usual process of human contact, but by close observation of books and objects. Perhaps this is why they emerged from the process with the inner soul of Japan untainted. It also explains why today the *gaijin* ("foreigner" in Japanese) find the Japanese so much like themselves, yet so different in their core.

MEIJI RESTORATION In 1867 the Emperor Komei died and his 15-year-old son took over as the Emperor Meiji, who was to rule Japan in its great golden era of growth and modernization for 45 years. In the following year, 1868, the great house of Tokugawa, which had provided Japan with fifteen *Shogun*, collapsed. Power went to the Imperial throne.

The Imperial family did not cling to their newfound power. In the spirit of the changing times, they set up a constitution in 1889, and the Imperial Diet, the governing body of Japan, in 1890. These were the first steps, which allowed Japan to mature into full democracy in 1946, under a different constitution.

MILITARY MIGHT

In the 87 years between 1854, when America forced Japan to open its doors, and the start of the Pacific War, Japan built up a fighting force.

In 1894, Japan fought against China, first in Korea and later on Chinese soil. To the world's surprise, Japan brought the Asian giant to its knees, exacting heavy compensation, which, much to Japan's resentment, Russia, France and Germany forced it to forego. The Emperor Meiji met the massive popular indignation with a plea that they should try "to bear the unbearable." In 1945, when Japan was forced to surrender in the Pacific War, Emperor Hirohito used the same words.

A Japanese general accepts surrender from a Russian commander during the Russo-Japanese War.

A lesser battle, the battle of the Sea of Japan against the Russian fleet during the Russo-Japanese War in 1905, had a greater historical impact than the war with China. In two days the Japanese destroyed the Russian Baltic fleet of 40 vessels. It was the first major victory of an Asian nation against a western one. It destroyed the myth of western invulnerability, and had far-reaching effects on the morale of all Asia, especially on the nationalists in colonialized territories.

In Japan there was a struggle between the militarists (those who wanted war) and the moderates (who did not). Charged with confidence from the Russo-Japanese War, the militarist elements in the country strengthened. There was much fighting overseas in China, Korea and Manchuria. In 1895 Japan had taken Formosa (Taiwan). In 1910 Japan annexed Korea, and ruled it for 35 years. Japan became a player in the international game of military power politics, and adopted an expansionist policy.

THE PACIFIC WAR

In July 1941 Japanese troops moved into Vietnam as part of Japan's China war strategy. The United States, Britain and Holland responded with an economic embargo on Japan. A series of talks ensued between the United States and Japan, which finally failed in November 1941. A Japanese fleet assembled at the Kurile islands northeast of Hokkaido set sail for the North Pacific. At dawn on December 7, Japanese planes crippled the American Pacific fleet anchored at Pearl Harbor in Hawaii.

The Japanese army swept down Hong Kong, Burma, Thailand, Malaya, Indonesia and the Philippines. The Japanese had estimated that it would take them three months to reach Singapore, but in fact they took only ten weeks.

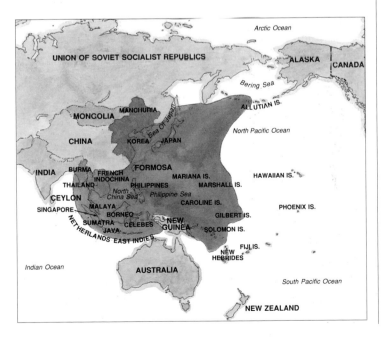

The Japanese empire in 1942 covered all of Southeast Asia.

The atomic-bombed cities of Hiroshima and Nagasaki were built up rapidly after the Pacific War, but the ruins of one building were left as a memorial and is known as the Atomic Bomb Dome.

THE PACIFIC WAR ENDS

The Battle of Midway in June 1942, when the Japanese were beaten in the Pacific, was the turning point in the Pacific War. In the three years that followed, Japan lost a series of battles. In February 1945, American forces landed on Iwojima. The Japanese fought to the last man on the doorstep of their homeland. The area of Iwojima is 8 square miles and it cost 20,000 American lives. The Japanese fought with the same ferocity through April, May and June in Okinawa, losing 39,000 men.

At 8:15 in the morning of August 6, 1945, an American Superfortress dropped an atomic bomb on Hiroshima. Russia attacked Japan on August 8. A second atomic bomb was dropped on Nagasaki on August 10. On August 13, Tokyo was attacked by over 1,500 planes from aircraft carriers cruising freely off the coast of Honshu. On August 14, American aircraft dropped thousands of leaflets over Tokyo, giving the Japanese the facts of messages exchanged between the Allies and the Japanese government.

Japan surrendered on August 15, 1945.

KAMIKAZE

Before the Pacific War, the Mongols attempted twice to conquer Japan, but failed because of heavy storms.

The Japanese regarded the typhoon as a divine intervention and called it *Kamikaze*, Wind of the Gods. In the Pacific War they applied this name to their force of daredevil suicide pilots. This painting shows university students, the cream of Japanese society, joining the *Kamikaze*.

THE OCCUPATION

The seven years of American occupation that followed, under General MacArthur, prepared the ground for an economic revival. For the second time in one hundred years, Japan underwent a transformation, from a war-torn country to one of the major industrial nations in the world.

Japan was rebuilt along the lines of the western world, but it was not a wholesale enforcement of western models. There was careful selection of what could be changed. There were misjudgements, too, as when the occupation administration tried to dissolve the powerful monopolistic *Zaibatsu* (literally, "economic group"), but altogether the changes helped to set the foundations of postwar Japan in areas such as the constitution, the legal system and the language.

GOVERNMENT

THE EMPEROR

JAPAN IS a democracy with a titular monarch, the Emperor. As in the United Kingdom, the monarch has no legal powers but commands great respect and symbolizes the head of the nation deep in the hearts of the Japanese.

The Imperial family of Japan descends from an unbroken lineage of nearly two thousand years. No other royal family in the history of man has ever been able to hold its position for so long. The origins of the Imperial family are obscure and mixed with myth, but historians generally agree that the first Emperor emerged at about the time of Christ. The family has for a long time laid claim to divine origin, and (like the English monarch) held a role of religious leadership, but these were clearly renounced on New Year's Day, 1946.

The Imperial family has survived the power struggles of feudal Japan because the military men who controlled the land always retained the titular head of their nation. Throughout the centuries, the family has been a quiet and stabilizing influence on Japan. It has also been closely connected with the arts.

Opposite: **Emperor Akihito and Empress Michiko. On his accession to the throne, January 7, 1989, the era of the new Emperor was designated** *Heisei* **("Peace and Concord").**

Above: **The Imperial crest. In historical times, the family crest helped warriors to tell friend from foe during arm-to-arm combat.**

DEMOCRACY AND THE GOVERNMENT

Japan was the first Asian country to introduce a parliamentary system. The Japanese had a unique opportunity to study what was happening all around the world, without the fetters of colonial rule, and select for themselves the system they wanted.

The first constitution, introduced in 1885, did not give power to the people; the Emperor still had ultimate control. However, it did lay the foundation for future democracy. Today, Japan is administered under a constitution which was completely redrafted by the American occupation administration in 1947. Coming into force in May 1947, Japan's second constitution retained the monarchy but subjected it to the will of the people.

The Parliament is made up of two legislative chambers known as the Diet. The House of Representatives, with 512 members, has a maximum term of 4 years. The House of Councillors, with 252 members, serves a 3-year term. In practice, general elections have occurred every two years. The House of Councillors has been dominated by the ruling party and has tended to ratify decisions as a matter of course. The chief executive of the Diet is the Prime Minister who is elected by the Diet. He is usually the leader of the majority party.

Japan is divided into 47 districts called prefectures. There are city, town and village assemblies for local administration.

The Diet in session.

THE MAJOR POLITICAL PARTIES IN JANUARY 1988

Party	Representatives	Councillors
Liberal Democratic Party	302	144
Japan Socialist Party	86	42
Komeito (Clean Government Party)	57	23
Democratic Socialist Party	29	12
Japan Communist Party	27	16
New Statesmen's Club (Tax Payers Party)	–	4
Niin Club	–	3
Salaried-Workers' New Party	–	3
Independents	5	4
Vacancies	6	1
TOTAL	512	252

THE LEGAL SCENE

The Supreme Court is in principle an organ to counterbalance the powers of the Diet and the Cabinet. The 14 Justices of the Supreme Court are, however, appointed by the Cabinet for 10-year terms and there has never been any major confrontation between these three centers of power. Under the Supreme Court there are eight High Courts and below these the district courts, one for each prefecture except Hokkaido, which has four.

Japanese law is framed in written codes, introduced in the 19th century, which are referred to but not upheld rigidly. There is no jury system and the procedure in a Japanese courtroom is more subdued and less dramatic than that of a typical American or European one. The low level of litigation in Japan is reflected in the fact that there is one lawyer to 9,000 people in Japan, compared to the United States where there is one lawyer to 400 people.

There are no legal enforcement treaties with other countries. If there were a legal dispute between, say, a Canadian and a Japanese on a contract written under Canadian law, the Canadian would not be able to enforce it unless the Japanese party had assets in Canada.

Bright yellow caps of junior schoolchildren alert drivers to children crossing roads. It is a practice to place a bin of yellow plastic flags on either side of a pedestrian crossing. The pedestrian stretches out the flag horizontally in front of him while crossing, then places it in the bin on the other side.

DEFENSE

The 1947 constitution had a "no-war" clause (Article 9) as one of the requirements of the MacArthur government. In 1953, however, U.S. Vice-President Nixon, speaking in Tokyo, stated that his country had been wrong to include Article 9 in the constitution.

Firemen giving a display of their community role, in traditional costume.

The Japanese government realizes the full implications of living under the United States' defense umbrella and of being left behind in military technology. In 1954 Self Defense Forces were set up with the Police Reserve Force as a base. Today there are 155,000 men in their ground force, 44,000 in the airforce and 44,000 in the navy. Until 1986 Japan had limited its defense expenditure to 1% of the GNP, but since its GNP is very high, the sum is substantial.

THE POLICE

Japan has a large police force, about one officer to 30 households. It has one of the lowest crime rates in the world. However, small extremist groups exist which oppose the law with fanatical intensity.

ECONOMY

THE MIRACLE ECONOMIC MACHINE

JAPAN'S ECONOMY grew out of the rubble of the Second World War, which ended in 1945. Forty-one years later, in 1986, the per capita income of Japan overtook that of the United States of America to become the highest in the world.

In the 1980's, Japan became the nation investing the most money overseas every year. Japanese multinational corporations are building factories all over the world. Japanese exports are everywhere. The world's largest financial institutions, the largest steelmakers, the largest shipbuilders, the largest consumer electronics firms are all in Japan.

This achievement is remarkable since Japan has no oil or mineral resources. About 40% of the Gross Domestic Product is in manufacturing, yet almost all the raw materials are imported from the United States, Canada, Australia and Southeast Asia. Japan imports 95% of the iron ore, tin and copper it needs. It is also the world's largest importer of coal, natural gas and oil.

Opposite: **Ginza, the "center of the center" of Tokyo city, is the most stylish and expensive shopping district of Japan.**

Below: **A Tokyo street.**

THE JAPANESE WORKER

The Japanese are quick to pick up good ideas, take them apart, improve on them, then market them. The English invented the pocket calculator but the Japanese flooded the market with better models. The French invented a train that ran at 125 miles per hour on an air cushion, and the Japanese went one better: a train that would do 185 miles per hour with magnetic levitation. Japan has overtaken the world in marketing technologically new products partly because of industrial strategies and partly because of the discipline and full commitment of its workers.

The working population represents a larger proportion of the total population than in most western countries. The proportion of working women is also high. Japan has a very large percentage in the service industries, about 57%. There are no major trade union problems. The common goal of more profits for the company is the base on which disputes are resolved.

Behind the efficiency of the Japanese workers is the fact that they have a very high average level of education. About 95% continue their education beyond the compulsory basic schooling. In the United Kingdom, the figure is approximately 40%.

Japan's economic success has, ironically, brought on economic and political problems. Many countries view Japan with suspicion as intruders with their export products and their overseas manufacturing. Fortunately, Japanese workers have a resilience and self-control born out of a history of struggles against natural calamities such as earthquakes and typhoons. This, and their inclination to look for a compromise, out of reasonableness and respect for the opinions of others, will ensure that Japan retains its economic position for many more years.

Opposite: **Sorting out the *ayu* fish. Fish is an important part of the Japanese diet and fishing ports are to be found all along the coasts of the Japanese islands.**

Quotas and restrictions on imports of Japanese automobiles, imposed by other countries, have given rise to this problem: thousands of automobiles waiting at docks to be shipped out.

JAPANESE AUTOMOBILE PRODUCTION*

Toyota Motor	30
Nissan Motor	20
Mazda Motor	10
Mitsubishi Motors	9
Honda Motor	9
Suzuki Motor	6
Isuzu Motors	5
Fuji Heavy Industries	5
Daihatsu Motor	5
Others	1

Percentage of total production in 1985

KEY ECONOMIC FACTS

- 40% of the Gross Domestic Product is from manufacturing.
- Unemployment was only 2.86% in 1986.
- Inflation was 2% in 1986.
- The labor pool of 60 million is a bigger proportion of population than in any western country.
- Japan is deficient in raw materials and relies heavily on imports.
- Japan is the world's largest importer of coal, natural gas and oil.
- Japan is the world's largest net importer of timber.
- Although Japan is 70% self-sufficient in foodstuffs, it has been the world's largest importer of fish since 1978.
- 95% continue education after schooling, compared to 40% in the U.K.

TRADE*

Top Ten Exports	*Top Ten Imports*
Road vehicles	Crude petroleum
Iron and steel	Natural gas
Scientific instruments	Electrical machinery
Telecommunications equipment	Petroleum products
Consumer electronics equipment	Coal
Chemicals	Non-ferrous metals
Office equipment	Fish and fish products
Ships	Wood and lumber
Power-generating equipment	Iron ore
Synthetic fabrics	Transport equipment

* These are 1985 figures. The U.S. was Japan's largest trading partner in 1985, supplying about 20% of its imports and taking about 37% of Japan's exports.

THE JAPANESE

THE JAPANESE are a Mongoloid sub-group, that is, they generally have yellowish skin, epicanthic (slanted) eyes, prominent cheekbones and black hair.

The origin of the race is controversial. There is a theory that Japanese were living on the Japanese islands from the Stone Age. Another suggests that since the early Stone Age there has been an eastward migration on the Asian continent, the farthest point reached being Japan. When Japan was separated from the mainland the Japanese race developed out of mixed migrants from China, Manchuria and Korea. Another theory is that there could have been migrants from the Oceanic or Malay regions.

AINU

One thing is clear, however: before the migrants arrived, a race called the Ainu lived in Japan. The Ainu are markedly non-Mongoloid, with the Caucasoid features of fair skin, abundant body hair, rounded eyes and flatter cheekbones. Recently, the theory that the Ainu were Caucasoid broke down with the discovery that they lack certain genes present in Caucasians. Over the centuries the Japanese drove the resisting Ainu northward to Hokkaido, where they live today.

The Ainu religion is animistic, one which believes all natural objects, such as animals, trees and stones, possess a spirit or soul. The bear plays a prominent role. Many Shinto rites are derived from Ainu rituals and a few Ainu place names, including Mt. Fuji, form part of the Japanese vocabulary.

Ainu girl of Hokkaido.

Uniforms are to be seen everywhere in Japan. Navy blue is the color of high school uniforms. These first-year high school students appear to be a little uncomfortable with their new collars.

JAPANESE CHARACTER

The Japanese are a very disciplined people whose society is divided into many compact groups. The attraction of a group and the desire to be immersed in a group is a basic part of Japanese character. The Japanese have to belong to a unit—such as a family—because it gives them a sense of security. They surrender their individuality to a large extent in exchange for the security of belonging to a group.

The basic unit is the home, as in most human societies. But although they retain the bond of the family or extended family all through life, the Japanese go farther and transfer this bond to almost all other spheres of their lives: school, university and work. In the legal field, Japanese advocates refer to the groups they belong to as the *mura* (village).

Strong attachments to groups have disadvantages. Emotions can be raised to exclude outsiders, even to the extent of forgetting the wider or umbrella group to which one also belongs. Conforming to styles and rituals can stifle individualism and the group leader could extract blind

obedience, exploiting the group for selfish ends. It is also possible to be locked into a group all one's life.

PROS AND CONS OF THE GROUP SYSTEM The disadvantages of group compactness can be seen in many areas of Japanese life. There is poor cooperation between the three different Buddhist organizations. Research teams made up of experts from different universities do not work out successfully in Japan. The merger of two of the largest breweries was prevented by the blind loyalty of employees to their company and their total faith in its management style. There is no "all-Japan" intellectual journal because several attempts to get various intellectual groups to work together have failed.

There are also advantages in group loyalty. The Japanese have learned over the years to extract maximum human effort through the spirit of compact teams. It is one of the most important reasons for their industrial success.

Neither do group leaders bully their teams or bulldoze their ideas forcibly over them. They have an almost paternal sense of responsibility for their group members and a constant awareness that everyone must play a part in decision-making to ensure that the group stays united.

RELATIONSHIPS

Strong cohesive forces operate within the Japanese group to weld it together. These are the *oyabun-kobun, sempai-kohai* and *doryo* relationships built up from early childhood.

An *oyabun-kobun* relationship is fostered very early between parent and child.

Oyabun-kobun is the parent-child relationship. It is stronger in Japan than in most other countries. Not only is the respectful attitude of the child to the parent fostered but the responsibility of the parent is equally emphasized.

Sempai-kohai is the senior-junior relationship. It is a powerful force that tempers the enthusiasm and hotheadedness of youth and keeps seniors in close touch with the thoughts and feelings of their juniors.

Doryo is the comradeship that results from being in the same college or university. It describes an emotion that is carried all through life in Japan, a beefed-up version of the British "Old School Tie" or American League Fellowships.

THE HIERARCHICAL SOCIETY The *oyabun-kobun* and *sempai-kohai* relationships put everyone on a series of steps: one is a parent and also a child, a *sempai* or *kohai* under different circumstances. These relationships arrange Japanese people in a series of layers, making it a hierarchical society. Everyone is ranked. The ranking gives every member of the community a proper place. It is a solution to the conflicts of competition, ambition and envy; if one's position is fixed and clear, these feelings are defused.

How do the Japanese resolve the "unequalness" that is part of a hierarchical system? Quite simply, the ranking is completely accepted in their hearts. Many other societies are split into layers and layers of levels and ranks. With the Japanese it is a deep-seated belief that spills over into other areas. The Japanese have a tendency to rank everything: universities, products and skills, for example. It comes with the desire to obtain all things *ichiryu* (first-class) if it can be afforded. In a way it is a striving for top quality.

SOCIAL MOBILITY The groups and pre-ordained levels are almost exclusive, but there are ways out of the system, opportunities to move in and out of groups, and up and down the ladder of ranks. The system imposes complicated ways to cross barriers, so that only the exceptional individual can climb over hurdles which the ordinary person is not permitted to surmount.

The Japanese *sempai-kohai* relationship is an important one. Every Japanese speaks of his or her *sempai*, a kind of personal guide. In a few years, these children will speak of their very own *sempai*.

A SENSE OF DUTY

All Japanese are conscious of their obligations. The obligation to return favors received, of doing the right thing for one's group or *sempai* (senior) is so complex that several words are required to distinguish the shades of difference—words such as *gimu*, *giri* and *on*. To the Japanese, doing one's duty is of the utmost importance.

"SAVING FACE"

Intertwined with the sense of duty and the *sempai-kohai* (senior-junior) relationship is the concept of personal image or "face," and the emotions and behavior it inspires. One must treat one's *sempai* with reverence and be gentle with one's *kohai*, always conscious of their feelings. Disgracing oneself affects them, too, and causes them shame. Appearances and "face" have to be maintained at all times.

This means that the inner self has to be suppressed or masked. Thus Japanese avoid giving a clear answer that commits them fully, and shrink from any direct confrontation. It is not shiftiness or deceit. It is necessary to use masks to keep interpersonal relationships smooth and unruffled. They describe their "split personality" with two words: *tatemae* is the façade (what appears in front, the external image), and *honne* is the real root (the true, inner self).

THE REVENGE OF THE 47 *RONIN*

A story to illustrate the Japanese sense of duty.

Lord Kira, a great *daimyo* (chieftain), had to instruct Lord Asano in the etiquette for a special ceremony. Unfortunately, the gifts Lord Asano offered to Lord Kira in exchange for the instruction fell short of expectations. On the big day, to his unbounded horror, Lord Asano was not dressed correctly. He drew his sword and attacked Lord Kira, wounding him on the forehead.

In great shame, Lord Asano dressed for *seppuku,* said farewell to Oishi, his trusted retainer, and killed himself. Since he had no heir, his estate was confiscated and his retainers became *ronin*—"wave men" or *samurai* drifting without a lord to serve. The *ronin*, led by Oishi, had to avenge their master's humiliation. The full burden of unfulfilled obligation hung on them. At a meeting, Oishi selected 47 *ronin*. They made a blood pact and the vendetta began.

It was a complicated plan. All Tokyo was expecting some move, so first Lord Kira had to be thrown off the scent. The 47 *ronin* frequented the worst drinking houses to give the impression that they had lost all pride and honor. Oishi divorced his wife and let his sword rust. One *ronin* killed his father-in-law, another sold his wife as a prostitute to get funds, while the sister of a third was sent to work in Lord Kira's household as a maid.

On the fateful night, Oishi threw a party for Lord Kira's guards at which they all got drunk. The *ronin* raided Lord Kira's stronghold and rushed to his room. He was not there, but his bed was still warm. They spread out and searched. Peeping into an outhouse, they saw a man crouching inside. One *ronin* lunged at him, driving his spear through the wooden wall, but when he withdrew it there was no blood on the blade.

Actually, it was Lord Kira and the spear *had* wounded him, but he had wiped the blood off the sword with his *kimono* sleeve. The *ronin* burst into the outhouse and recognized him from the scar left on his forehead by Lord Asano's sword. They demanded that he commit *seppuku* at once but the coward refused. They cut off Lord Kira's head and set out in a procession, with the sword and the head, to Lord Asano's grave. The *ronin* had paid off their obligation.

BODY LANGUAGE

Japanese are extremely observant and send out the most subtle body-language messages. They call this *haragei* or the "belly feel," listening to the subconscious voice that interprets the minutest sign: a twitch of a facial muscle, an eye movement or a gesture.

When two Japanese meet the process begins with the ritual of bowing. The angle of the bow, the delay before straightening up, the number of bows—all add up to outline the positions they are taking in relation to each other, just as one reads and shows attitudes with the jutting out chin, folded arms, slight dip of the head from the neck or firm handclasp. In Japanese novels, reaction of the eyes is described much more often than in western writing.

APPARENT INDISCIPLINE The Japanese are a highly disciplined people, yet sometimes their behavior appears shockingly wild and uncontrolled. They get quite drunk in public; at festivals they seem unrestrained in their enjoyment; and they publicly enjoy various forms of pornography.

This behavior stems from the Japanese philosophy of life. To the Japanese, suppression of a tendency to pleasure is unnatural. Yet, at the same time, every pleasure must be relegated to its proper place, as a distraction from the serious business of life. Seen in that perspective, the soul is not corrupted by occasional excesses.

WOMEN IN JAPAN

Women have not yet broken away from tradition and achieved equality in Japan. For many years the authorities have tried to elevate women's status, but there exists an odd mixture of progress and traditionalism with regard to women in Japanese society.

Throughout the centuries they have pushed themselves forward to challenge and match male dominance. There are few countries in the world in which women have played such a major role in the arts. Chinese records of Japanese history describe a queen, Himiko, who brought an end to the wars between the small states in Japan and established a unified nation. It is recorded that her state was "Yamatai" and that when she died one hundred slaves were buried with her.

Two young girls, one in modern dress, the other in a simple *kimono*. Another generation may bring them greater freedom from their traditional role.

The woman in Japan is relegated to a subservient role. It would be unusual for a Japanese man to open the door for a Japanese woman or let her go through the door first. Her place is the home, and there she is given some power. The Japanese husband gives his wife his entire salary and she budgets for the household, giving him pocket money. (Japanese companies have circumvented this traditional domestic control to some extent by keeping salaries low and handing out a large bonus twice a year. The Japanese husband does not surrender the bonus to his wife.)

There have been exceptional women in the last two decades who have run large companies, written bestsellers and led the field in fashion design but the average Japanese woman, however steeped in western lifestyle when single, reverts to a traditional role when she marries.

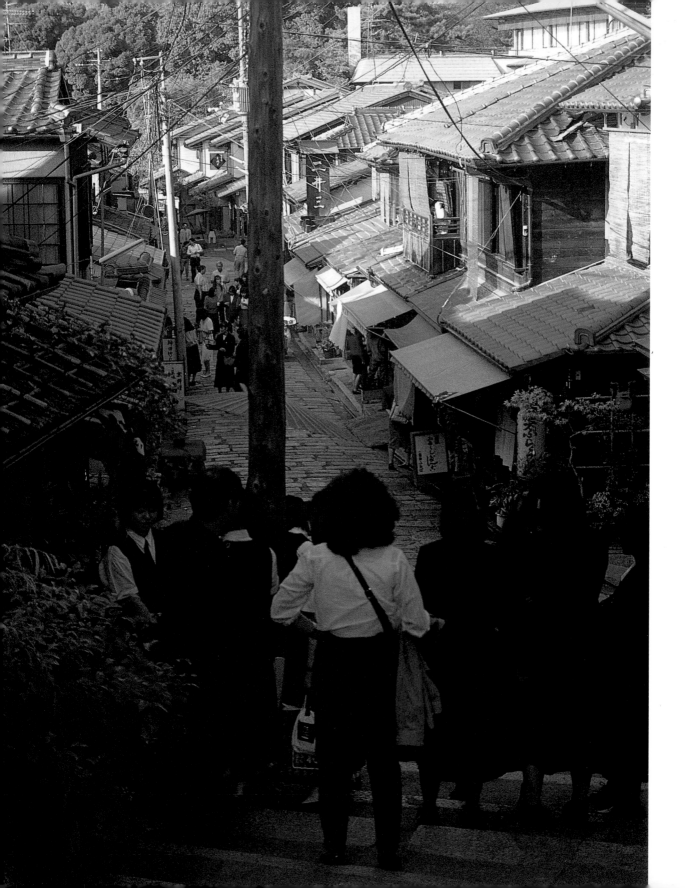

LIFESTYLE

EVOLVING A LIFESTYLE

THE DISCIPLINED LIFESTYLE of the Japanese evolved out of their physical environment. The harsh climate of cold winters and heavy snowfalls in the north, hot summers, typhoons, and above all the earthquakes and volcanoes, have made them rugged and ready to adapt their living conditions to changing forces.

The Japanese once lived in small paper houses that could be rebuilt easily after earthquakes and fires. They depended greatly on protein from the sea, but slow transportation inland made them resort to eating seafood with sour, fermented rice to mask the smell of decaying fish. In the north they learned to pickle vegetables to last through long winters. As the population grew, overcrowding became a major problem.

In essence, Japanese lifestyle has not changed for centuries.

The pleasures which the Japanese have, they enjoy immensely, if only for short respites. They add a glint of beauty to the everyday and the mundane. One example of this is their packaging. There are rules and forms of how to wrap and embellish a present. As important as the choice of the offering is the visual pleasure given with the gift; the symbolic communication of the paper or silk wrapper, its folding, color, pattern, the added decoration that gives the subtle touch of completeness.

Another example is the way food is arranged and served. The visual experience adds to the enjoyment of a meal: the sizzle more than the steak!

Opposite: **Most Japanese cities were built as castle towns, where life centered on the castle of the** *daimyo* **(chieftain). Away from industrial zones, these places dream on, disturbed only occasionally by visiting Japanese and other tourists.**

Below: **A quirky way of presenting shrimp.**

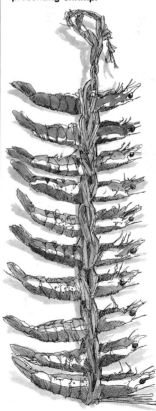

TRADITIONAL AND MODERN HOMES

Housing is a great problem in the cities, where 80% of Japan's population (123 million) live. Osaka and Tokyo, the largest cities, together house about 25 million. Japan used to rely greatly on fishing and farming, and in 1960 about 50% of the population worked on the land or in fishing.

The houses are small but, as they have always been small, the Japanese accept the minimal space standards. With urban sprawl and limited high-rise housing development (since Japan lies in the earthquake belt), many are forced to live one to two hours, by train, from the city centers.

The traditional Japanese house has no tables or chairs. The Japanese sit on straw mats called *tatami* and it is usual to measure house and room

in terms of the *tatami*, each about 3 by 6 feet. Bedding consists of light mattresses and blankets which are put away into cabinets every morning so as not to clutter the small rooms. Since Japanese often sit on the floor, shoes are taken off as soon as they enter the house and house slippers are worn. House slippers are changed for bathroom slippers before entering the bathroom.

Today, tables and chairs are often used and some houses are built with western and Japanese sections.

Japanese houses do not have fireplaces to give a focus to the room as in the west. The focal point in a

Top: **Slippers (*surippa*) came to Japan from the west. Note the two sets, outdoor and home footwear.**

Bottom: **Typical bedroom with a mattress that can be rolled neatly out of the way in daytime.**

Japanese living room is an alcove called the *tokonoma*. In the old days, little stoves covered with blankets warmed feet and legs. These warmers are still used in the country, but in the cities electric fires are the norm at home and commercial buildings are centrally heated. A typical Japanese home in the city has all the electrical conveniences which one takes for granted in a western home.

Aerial view of congested Tokyo.

In the country, where space is not a problem, construction standards and environmental conditions of houses are well below those of houses in the cities. A nation that has led the world in mass-producing articles to allow one to get more out of life at any income level has left the country folk generally living in the technology of the 1950's and 1960's.

Above: *Geisha* means "artist" and *geisha* girls are artists of social graces. A *geisha* studies dancing and singing, make-up and dress, flower arranging and the ritual tea ceremony. She can be recognized by her distinctive *kimono*, *obi* (sash), platform sandals and exotically made-up face.

Above right: The *kimono* is preferred for ceremonial occasions by both bride and female guests. The groom may wear a western suit, or, as shown in the picture, a *haori-hakama*—long pleated trousers resembling a divided skirt. The family crest figures on sleeves, and the back and front of the jacket. Male guests prefer the western suit.

JAPANESE DRESS

The Japanese dress with care and forethought. In fact, Japanese fashion design is now recognized as belonging to the realm of high fashion. Several designers have won international fashion awards. One of them, Hanae Mori (nicknamed "Iron Butterfly" because of the butterfly motif identifying her collections), has received France's most coveted cultural award, the Croix de Chevalier des Arts et des Lettres. Japanese dress has come a long way from the *kimono*.

The traditional *kimono*, a one-piece wraparound garment held in place at the waist by a sash, is, however, still the dress preferred for ceremonial occasions. One hardly sees the *kimono* these days, although the light evening *yukata*, which is like a *kimono*, is worn at home.

Western dress has replaced traditional wear to such an extent that in another generation the Japanese will need lessons on how to wear a *kimono*! Businessmen all wear dark lounge suits with white shirts. They use their version of English words for these: *sebiro* (from Savile Row) for the suit and *waishattu* for the white shirt.

Men and women who work in factories all wear uniforms. The general rule is that unless the employee has to present himself to customers, he wears a company uniform.

GOOD MANNERS

The Japanese have rules for almost every human activity and even today many of the old rules of correct behavior are faithfully observed. Take bowing for example: it has a whole series of set forms: the very deep, respectful bow, bowing when seated, how to position hands while bowing, the need to come to a stop before bowing rather than bowing in mid-stride…

Visiting rules are similar to those in English Victorian society: whom and when to visit, the proper entrance, refolding the towel offered to the visitor before putting it down, how to drink tea and eat cakes, polite leave-taking…

There are rules for gifts: the times of year when gifts are expected, when fans should be given, when pickles should be given, above all, the way they are wrapped, for, be the gift ever so thoughtful, one could still insult the receiver by not folding the paper correctly.

Rules also exist for weddings and funerals. One should never say *sayonara* (goodbye) to the bride and groom, for example, because the word is too final. One should never call on someone on the way home from attending a funeral.

Underlying all the forms of etiquette is the principle that nothing should be communicated directly. Symbols, hints and getting to the point in roundabout fashion are the characteristics of social intercourse in Japan. Saying the wrong thing directly could embarrass the other party, even if it is praise or flattery because both praise and flattery demand the correct response; otherwise, there is loss of face.

Above: **Bowing at the right angle.**

Below: **A *furoshiki*, or cloth wrapper.**

53

Shibuya is the satellite town for younger people. Well provided with burger joints and youthful entertainment, it is frequented by students.

RELAXATION

Although Japanese life is so strictly channeled into the grooves fixed by social norms, they have opportunities to break away from the restrictions of their patterned living.

For example, Japanese society condones getting drunk. Another form of social escape provided are the festivals. The Japanese let themselves go at their festivals. They let the drumbeats get to them; they sing and dance, pushing themselves physically, mixing freely, into the small hours of the morning.

People in Paris, London, Frankfurt or Los Angeles who meet visiting Japanese businessmen regularly, who have eaten and drunk with them, shown them the city lights and had pleasant and memorable evenings with them, often do not realize that behind the same polite, smiling, impassive faces are people who, on occasion, can run wild.

COURTSHIP

Western lifestyle is evident in all the Japanese cities, but subtle differences exist which are not obvious. Such is the case with social contact between young boys and girls, or between men and women.

Arranged meetings with a view to marriage still occur, but today after the meeting the young people are left to work it out themselves. Romantic love in the western sense is strong and will determine the match or mismatch decision. After this, an ingrained sense of duty will be the rock on which a marriage will develop and grow.

This does not mean that the Japanese are not romantic. There is a mixture of a traditional sense of duty and the romantic love of a married couple that their poets sang about. This is a somewhat restrained yielding to personal feelings, which is one of many escapes the Japanese lifestyle allows in the face of society's rigid discipline.

A gloomy, cold January day for these courting couples leaving a Shinto shrine.

55

THE FAMILY

The Japanese man gives his life to the company he works for; it is his focus, his real world. The woman gives hers to her home and family. Despite the influence of western ideas, these basics have not changed; nor will they change for a long time.

PARENTS The businessman father spends hardly any time with his family during the week. He leaves early and returns late, not because he is wining and dining until midnight but because he has a long distance to travel. An executive who goes home early every night loses status in the eyes of the neighbors, who will conclude that he is not important enough to entertain customers. The mother controls family expenditure, and thereby exerts her indirect influence on the household; but her role is clearly inferior to the man of the house.

CHILDREN Children spend their early years struggling with language.

Junior high examinations are highly competitive and parents send their children to *juku* or "cram" schools where they receive special tutoring. Fees are high and the pace intensive.

They have to learn different verbal languages for addressing superiors, equals and inferiors; and they also must learn important body languages. This is before they go to school, where they must master writing and reading approximately one hundred phonetic characters and the much more complex Chinese characters, of which they would know 1,850 by the time they leave school.

Appreciation of the arts is instilled in them. They study the beauty of brush strokes in calligraphy and painting. They are taken to scenic and historic places and learn *origami*, or the creation of forms in three dimensions through paper-folding. They sing, dance or learn to play a musical instrument.

Bright children will try to get into a university—a difficult ordeal, for the workload is huge, memories are stretched and perseverance is tested. If they succeed, they are set for life, as their lifestyle is determined by the university they go to. The Japanese brand people by their university, a tendency adopted from the western world but held with greater rigidity in Japan. Elementary students may enroll in private "cram" schools to help them qualify for a good high school, which in turn puts them on the road to a more reputable university.

TEENAGE TO ADULTHOOD In the cities teenagers and youths under thirty enjoy life. They have money to spend on clothes, records and tapes, motorcycles and things which generate the modern concept of fun. Japanese teenagers enjoy American music, television, movies and writing. Their parents felt the same in their teens but as they grew older

the cultural pull of the land of their ancestors brought them back to Japan. All the indications are that this will not change, though some doubt it.

The lifestyles of the young and the middle-aged are as different in Japan as they are all over the world. However, the disciplines of their upbringing, the cultural chasms between the Japanese and westerners exist, holding Japan back from irreversible "internationalism."

Below: **Teens gather in the Harajuku area of Tokyo every Sunday, when roads are blocked and the young people dance.**

Opposite: **Movie posters draw passers-by to the movie theater.**

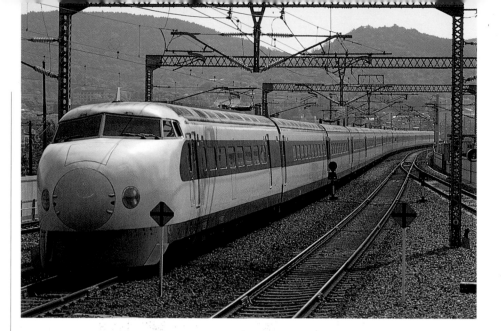

A "bullet" train can reach a maximum of 150 miles an hour, a boon to the commuting Japanese worker.

A TYPICAL DAY

The working day of a typical Japanese man begins very early. He lives many miles from the city where he works, and would probably take two buses and the suburban train, a journey of at least an hour and a half. He makes sure he gets in early.

The working day starts with an assembly. He and his workmates do some limbering-up exercises, sing the company song and may get a pep-talk from the manager before they report to their work stations.

He works with great concentration all day, putting heart and soul into every little operation, as is ingrained in him. He must not fail. He must not let his company down. Although he is only a factory worker, he sees the President quite often because the President walks through the factory regularly. He knows that if something disturbs him badly he can approach the President. Yet he will never do this without much deliberation and discussion with his workmates, because such an approach will have to be on behalf of the group.

When the day ends he will drop into a small bar for a beer or *sake* (Japanese rice wine) with his workmates. If he is a company executive he will have an expense account to use, not only for his customers but also for his staff. The company realizes that drinking together helps bring the team closer.

He will probably go to an *akachochin*, a red lantern bar. Here they

Picnicking under cherry blossoms is a favorite family outing in springtime.

may have a *karaoke* system (see page 46): everyone will have to do his turn, whether it is singing to recorded accompaniment or reciting a poem. They will have great fun, but he must watch the signs to ensure he upsets no one.

When the Japanese working man returns home, his wife gives him all her attention. This is changing, but very slowly. The ideal wife in the minds of Japanese men and women is the woman completely devoted to her family, who responds to every whim of her husband and very often of her children—her male children in particular.

During the weekend he takes his family out unless he is one of the very few who can afford to play golf. (If he has that privilege he will spend all the time he can on the golf course and play with fanatical enthusiasm.) Tennis, skiing, a short day trip to some historical or scenic place will be on top of the family list of preferences. There may be hundreds of people there but they will not mind. If there is a festival that weekend they will participate in it.

61

RELIGION

TWO RELIGIONS

RELIGION IS an integral part of Japanese life. Although it is ever-present, it does not interfere in everyday life. If asked whether she or he is religious, a Japanese will reply "no," yet will observe all the Shinto rites and visit Buddhist temples without being conscious of participating in anything special. In a country of about 123 million people, there are approximately 184,000 buildings of worship—that is an average of 670 persons per place of worship!

The primary religions are Shinto and Buddhism. It has been said that Shinto takes care of daily living while Buddhism takes care of the after-life. Most Japanese follow both religions without being concerned about which is right. It is an attitude that westerners find hard to understand. When J. Seward wrote, "The Japanese have tended to mold their religions to fit their way of life more than the reverse," he highlighted one aspect of the Japanese attitude toward religion.

Opposite: **The Kamakura Buddha.**

Below: **The Grand Shrine of Ise is the leading shrine of Shinto. It has preserved its form for over a thousand years, "renewed" every 20 years through being torn down and rebuilt.**

SHINTO

Shinto, literally "the way of the gods," does not have a clear principle or a definite family of deities. It is present in the belief held by the Japanese from the earliest times that there is a certain spiritual essence in all things, living or non-living, even in rocks, the wind, the sea and echoes. They call this *kami*. The Japanese character for *kami* means "above" or "superior." *Kami* is often translated as "god" but it does not really embody the western concept of god.

Right: **Shinto ceremony.**

Far right: **Tree of paper blessings. These are strips of paper picked by the worshiper through one of many means: it could be with the help of a bird or the result of shaking a bamboo container of "fortune sticks." The "blessing" is secured to a tree or gate, or some other structure in the temple grounds.**

SHRINES To the Japanese, the Emperor is a *kami*, but he is not God. Spirits of national heroes, famous scholars and officials, rivers, mountains, stands of trees or cliffs are *kami*. They install shrines to show their gratitude for protection and favors, and pray at these shrines for success.

The taboos are primitive and do not affect Japanese lives substantially. There are no rules of self-discipline. The Shinto belief is that man is born good and should therefore follow his natural impulses.

RITES AND SYMBOLS Shinto does not have the paraphernalia of most religions. Sticks, leaves and strips of paper are used for generally simple rituals. One essential feature of Shinto rites are the symbolic purification acts a Japanese performs before approaching a Shinto shrine—the washing of hands and mouth, for example. Shinto rituals are part of Japanese birth and wedding ceremonies, as well as a part of ceremonies for launching ships and laying foundation stones for new ventures.

SHINTO IN JAPANESE HISTORY

Shinto had been subject to manipulation in the past. Although the Shinto priests cleared some of the vagueness of their religion when Buddhism entered the country, Shinto could not compete with the elaborate Buddhist rituals, the well-defined Buddhist moral code, its philosophical approach, and, to some extent, the architecture, arts and food.

In 1700 there was a revival and, after the Meiji Restoration, the government employed Shinto as a unifying force. Financing was provided and Shinto became almost, though not quite, a state religion. In 1884 the government thought it necessary to declare that it was not a state religion but a cult. It forbade the Shinto priests to preach their religion.

In December 1945 the American occupation administration persuaded the Japanese government to stop financing Shinto, breaking the link between the religion and the State. Shinto temples moved into business ventures, selling off part of their land or using it and their funds to invest in temple parking lots, kindergartens, wedding halls and agricultural enterprises.

Shinto survived and today there are about 100,000 Shinto priests in about 90,000 shrines.

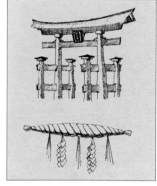

Symbols of Shinto shrines, the *torii*, a graceful gateway, and the *shimenawa*, a straw festoon fixed around trees in the shrine compound to mark the sacred ground.

Above: **Jizou Buddha, the common people's Buddha, dressed as offering to the gods. Such a doll is bought, adorned and offered with a wish—this one is probably for a baby. The selling of Jizou Buddha is big business in Japan.**

Above right: **Smoke is blown to bless a son.**

BUDDHISM

Buddhism came to Japan in A.D. 552. It brought to Japan a philosophy of life that was both simple and intellectually satisfying. It was clear in its principles, in its taboos, and yet impressive in its rituals, art and architecture. Buddhism swept across Japan to fill a vacuum left by Shinto.

Buddhism penetrated Japanese society at its highest levels. Prince Shotoku (574–622), whose portrait appears on some yen notes, persuaded his mother, the Empress Regent Suiko, that Buddhism did not conflict with Shinto. It was exalted to a State religion.

Buddhism only became popular with the masses from about the 13th century. It influenced both the philosophy and food of Japan, but it never replaced Shinto. Buddhism contributed to the way the Japanese regard death—as an accepted part of the divine scheme of all things. Buddha's dying words, "All things are transitory" has made a deep impression on the character of the Japanese.

ZEN

When the Japanese absorb a foreign concept, they add to it, or give it a Japanese character. Two monks, Eisai (1141–1215) and Dogen (1200–1235), brought Zen Buddhism from China. The essence of Zen is: "Look within yourself; you yourself are the Buddha." It is a philosophy of meditation and its fundamental belief is that in every human being there is something precious and divine.

Zen Buddhism appealed to the Japanese. They organized a Buddhist movement, known as Nichiren Shoshu or the Soka Gakkai.

Nichiren (1222–1282) was a colorful and outstanding monk who placed his whole faith in the *Lotus Sutra* book of Buddhism. He appealed to the common man by linking Buddhism with natural life. His predictions of future events won him fame, particularly when he foresaw the Mongol invasion of Japan. He took a clear stand by attacking other religions.

A monk begs for monetary donations. Some other sects do the same for food.

The Soka Gakkai promoted Zen Buddhism with almost military zeal. It went on a campaign of *shakabuku*, literally, to shatter and subdue, and used psychology to convert the unconvinced. It appealed to the lower rungs of society by offering personal dignity and self-importance. The Soka Gakkai has moved beyond Japan to other countries in Asia, and to America. In Japan, it started the Komeito (Clean Government Party or Value-creating Learned Society) but it does not play a major role in the party today.

CHRISTIANITY

Less than 1% of the Japanese are Christians. As with such minorities, the force of the majorities developed in them an instinct for survival. The Japanese Christians have a history of faith and perseverance that is quite remarkable.

Francis Xavier and other Christian missionaries came to Japan in 1594. By 1635 they had between 200,000 and 300,000 converts. There were factors that stood in their favor and the counting of true Christians is questionable, but the fact is that a large and powerful Christian community was established.

Christianity reached the highest levels of the *Shogun* administration, but inter-denomination rivalry weakened the foundations the pioneers had laid. Christians were eventually persecuted and the struggle reached a climax in the siege and massacre of 30,000 at Shimabara in 1638. To this day, historians argue about the religious and political aspects of the Christian resistance.

Japan isolated itself from the world after that, but when missionaries were allowed in after America opened the doors in 1857, a church was built in Nagasaki and four thousand Japanese Christians came to the church to rejoice. They had kept their faith alive and secret for 225 years.

RELIGIOUS ORGANIZATIONS IN JAPAN

These figures are of the number of religious organizations in Japan and their membership in 1985. They show the similar numbers of Shinto and Buddhist members. Another peculiar feature is that the total number of members exceeds the population of Japan (121 million in 1985); this is because many Japanese are registered both as Shinto and as Buddhist.

Religion is not taught in schools, and marriage between members of different religions is not a problem. In fact, it is not unusual for newlyweds to report their wedding to their ancestors at the family altar, have a Christian wedding ceremony, then honeymoon around Shinto shrines and Buddhist temples.

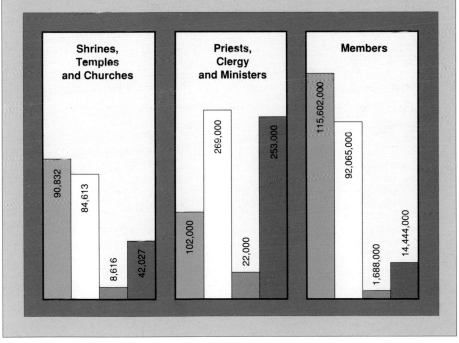

"Japanese culture has no conception of a God existing abstractly, completely separate from the human world."

— *Chie Nakane*

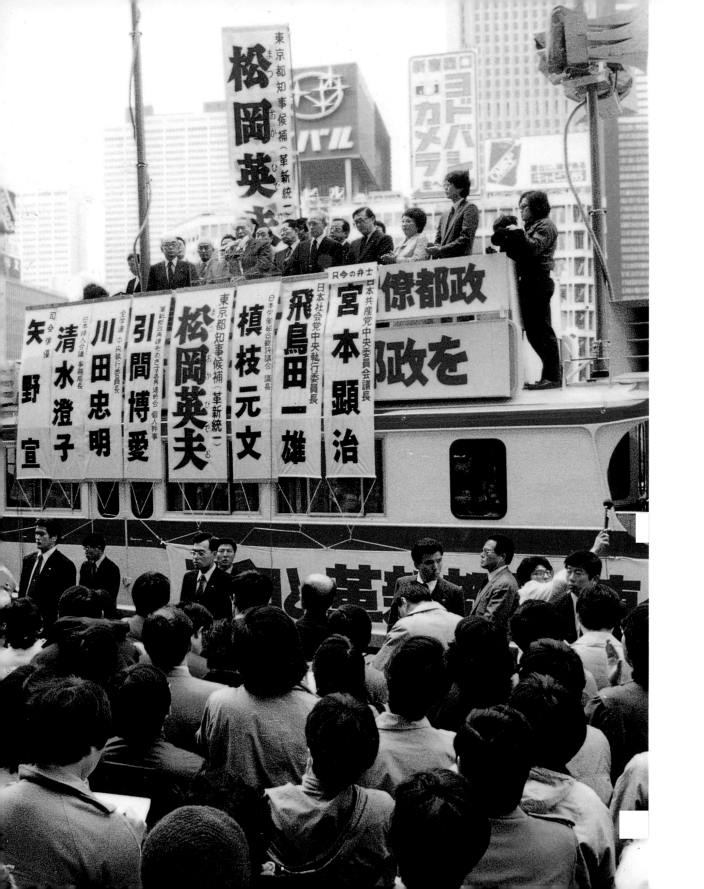

LANGUAGE

JAPANESE IS a well developed language similar to European languages in grammar and to Chinese in script. It is much clearer than Chinese. For example, the words *wa* and *o* are always used after the subject and the object respectively.

Tenses are precise. Nouns, however, are not varied, and there is no difference between the plural and the singular. Nor is there usually any difference between "he" and "she." Japanese places the adjective after the noun it qualifies, a structure used in Malay, French and Italian.

SOCIAL TONES

The need to be continuously aware of one's position is carried to the extreme. The pronouns "you" and "I" have many variants to reflect deference for age and status. Words are selected to reflect the status *vis à-vis* speaker and listener at all times.

Different verbs, verb endings and ways of using the same words must be considered. The verb "to come," for example, ranges from the crude *koi*, shouted to children and army privates, to the soft *irrashaimase* ("please come in") one hears on entering a Japanese restaurant. The verb "to be" has a similar range. The most polite form is *de gozaimasu,* which is generally used in public announcements. Women always use the polite form. Girls have to learn to change from rough and simple children's language to the softer, polite adult female form.

INDIRECTNESS In speech, the Japanese prefer to be indirect. American-style straight-from-the-shoulder frankness is considered rude. Conversational sentences are thus longer than in English. This indirectness often appears in the written form.

Opposite: **Political campaigns in Japan, like their counterparts in other countries, depend on the skillful use of language.**

Tachiyomi means "to stand and read."

VERBS

Verbs are often joined to make new verbs. *Tachiyomi* is such a verb: *tachi* (to stand) and *yomi* (to read). It means "stand and read." The word filled a need to describe a common pastime and a common sight in bookshops. Verb-joining opens up possibilities for creative writers.

PRONUNCIATION

Japanese pronunciation is straightforward and clear. It is not a tonal language. There may be two or three meanings of the same sounds but the context in most cases makes this meaning clear. There are no words ending in consonants (except *ng*), and no diphthongs.

There are no dialects. Pronunciation and a certain amount of word usage differ across the islands but there is only one Japanese language.

SOUNDS OF WORDS		PRONUNCIATION
There are a great many examples of onomatopoeia (words with sounds that reflect their meaning) in Japanese.		*a* as in art
		ai as in aisle
		e as in get
ha-ha	gasp, pant	*ei* as in veil
ki-ki	squeaky	*g* (always hard)
goro-goro	rumbling	as in go
pota-pota	water dripping	*i* as in tin
kusu-kusu	giggle	*n* as in sing
bechakucha	chatterbox	*o* as in pole
		u as in rude

Japanese is not an easy language to learn. Take, for example, the verb "to bring" which has two forms: one for things (*motte-kiru*), the other for people (*tsurete-kiru*). But it is not quite as clear as this. One uses the "people" verb (*tsurete-kiru*) if one brings a dog. If a bird or goldfish is brought then the "thing" verb (*motte-kiru*) is used; not because they are carried, since bringing a baby still requires the "people" verb (*tsurete-kiru*)!

"ADOPTED" ENGLISH

Many English words incorporated into the Japanese language have been distorted from their original meaning. A pre-war ladies' fashion word "two-piece," for example, was transported to Japan, where the *one-pisu* was devised to describe a dress. They took the English "glass" and reduced its ambiguity by using *garasu* for plate glass and *gurasu* for drinking glass.

Often the original word is unrecognizable. "Juice" becomes *jeeyusu*, and because they have no *l*, "lemon" becomes *remon*. "Lemon juice" thus becomes *remon jeeyusu*. English words are shortened: *biru* means "building;" *sutando* means "standard lamp." Some other examples are *bonasu* (bonus), *chi-zu* (cheese), *gorofu* (golf) and *maika* (my car).

JAPANESE EXAMPLES

NAMES Most Japanese girls' names, not all, end with *ko,* which means "little" or "child." Typical names are Yukiko (*yuki* means snow), Hanako (*hana* means flower) and Sachiko (*sachi* means happiness).

The surname is placed first, but, almost without exception, businessmen overseas reverse this order. Thus TAKAHASHI Kintaro becomes Kintaro TAKAHASHI on his overseas business card.

"MISTER" This is *San. San* is also Missus and Miss. A respectful version of "Mister" is *Sama.* It is hardly ever used today for individuals. It is used for addressing groups much in the same way that one says "Ladies and Gentlemen" in English, or when referring to a god: *kamisama.*

"BELLY" The Japanese place the seat of emotions in the stomach, as some English expressions, like "gut-feeling," do. In Japanese one says "the stomach is hungry." The "stomach standing" means "to be angry;" "not showing one's stomach" means concealing one's real intentions; to "probe the stomach" is to sound out someone's thoughts; to "cut the stomach and speak" is to be open and frank.

Harakiri (the literal, vulgar meaning is "belly-slitting") is suicide by cutting the stomach open. The deeper implication is the baring and bleeding of one's soul. In fact, those committing *harakiri* seldom die from the disembowelling cut. Death usually comes from a sword blow to the neck delivered by the ritual attendant (see page 45).

GESTURES To emphasize oneself, Japanese point to the nose, not the heart. When counting with fingers, they start with the open hand and bring each finger down to the palm in turn.

Opposite right: **All characters with the tree character have something to do with trees or wood. This allows limited guessing of meanings of characters one does not know. Some characters include another character which may have no relevance to the whole character meaning: it is there for the pronunciation.**

Opposite left: **Kana and the Chinese characters from which they are derived.**

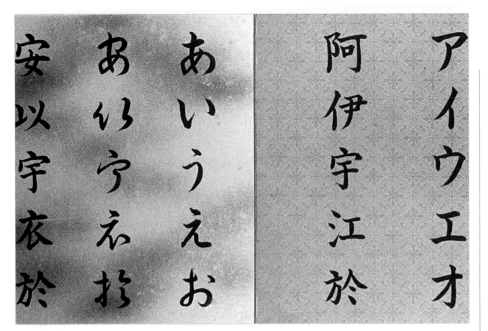

SCRIPTS

The Japanese adapted Chinese for their written language. Chinese characters first came to Japan through Korea, although some writing found in burial mounds suggests that written Chinese may have come directly from China. Chinese characters are simplified drawings called ideograms. An example is given on the right.

KANA The Japanese simplified Chinese characters and devised two phonetic scripts of their own. The sounds are the same for both. These are the *hiragana* and the *katakana,* collectively known as *kana.* The Chinese characters they use are known as *kanji.* The Japanese script uses *kana* interspersed with *kanji* which may have one or more syllables. *Kanji* is complex and has contributed to Japan's education problems. The Japanese have been trying to reduce the number of *kanji* for many years. In 1946 the education ministry reduced it to 1,850 characters, but one has to know much more than these to read Japanese books today. Novelists do not limit their repertoire to 1,850 characters.

The removal of thousands of *kanji* from the official list gave rise to problems of surnames. It was as though the government of the United States of America decided that "Smith" was an obsolete word and deleted it from all official lists!

ARTS

JAPAN IS ONE of the very few countries in the world where the arts are appreciated not only by the intelligentsia but also by the masses. Appreciation of the arts is instilled in Japanese children from the earliest years at home. In upper secondary school, the arts are represented by twelve separate subjects: three levels each of music, fine arts, handicrafts and calligraphy.

VISUAL ARTS

The visual arts in particular are one of the pleasures of all Japanese. They range from landscape gardening, *ikebana* (flower arrangement), *bonsai* (growing of miniature trees), goldfish breeding, painting, pottery, stone carving, to dyeing of silk and textile printing, making swords, paper, lacquerware, kites, drums and musical instruments, dolls, masks, paper-folding and the architecture of buildings in wood. In Japan, the men and women skilled in visual arts are called "living national treasures."

Opposite: **Japanese sculpture has its roots in China and the subjects of pieces such as this one are influenced by Chinese symbolism.**

Below: **The growing of miniature trees through careful pruning is an art called** *bonsai*.

IKEBANA AND LANDSCAPE GARDENING

The emphasis in both art forms is on naturalism. The flower arranger and garden landscape designer get their inspiration from nature.

In *ikebana*, the art of Japanese flower arrangement, the flowing line is more important than color or form. It may be a fallen branch picked from the roadside, but if it has a beautiful shape or line, it can be the basis of an *ikebana* arrangement. Groups of flowers, no matter how striking in color or form, take second place.

Another interesting feature of *ikebana* is that materials used reflect the passage of time: the past (represented by full blooms, pods or dried leaves), the present (half-open blossoms or perfect leaves) and the future (buds). As in many other Japanese visual arts, the season plays a major role: fall would see a sparse arrangement and summer a full, spreading one.

Landscape gardening is represented by two basic forms: hilly and flat. Water is a vital part of both. It is represented by sandy waves in a dry landscape (made with sand, stones and rocks) and by a pool or stream in evergreen landscapes. The colors are stark and severe in dry landscapes: light sand, black or gray rocks and stones. "Natural" landscapes, on the other hand, may feature a pavilion, stone lanterns and pagodas, rocks and stones subtly placed to represent islands and hills, evergreens and *bonsai* (usually non-flowering), bridges and paths.

PAINTING

Every house hangs a *kamemono* (hanging thing) in the main room. Only one picture is hung, and this is changed every season. One is thus reminded by the picture of changes in one's own home and in the homes of friends.

Painting in Japan really started in the 7th century A.D., when the Korean monk, Doncho, introduced paper, the techniques of mixing colors and other innovations. Paintings were done on silk or paper without models or attention to true perspective. A short description of, or a reference to the painting, in the form of a poem, was part of the picture; the calligraphy with which this was written was a work of art in itself.

Buddhism had a strong influence on painting from the 8th century right through to the Kamakura period. In the Heian period large horizontal scroll paintings of the life of Buddha were produced. By the Kamakura period, painting had gone beyond landscapes, trees and flowers: animals, pictures of everyday life and some caricatures were being painted.

WOODCUTS

In the 18th century, the woodblock for printing became popular. Woodblock printing combined two skills: the artist's and the woodblock craftsman's. The skill of the woodblock craftsman allowed the reproduction of works of art at an affordable price.

One of the best known artists of that century was Utamaro Kitagawa (1754–1806). *A Book of Insects* was his first volume of prints. He also produced drawings of courtesans and lovers. Sharaku, another artist, was noted for his pictures of popular *noh* and *kabuki* actors.

Hokusai Katsushita (1760–1849) and Hiroshige Ando (1749–1858) were two very prominent woodcut artists. Hokusai Katsushita's best known works are *Thirty-six Views of Mt. Fuji, One Hundred Views of Mt. Fuji, Scenes of Edo (Tokyo) and the Sumida River*, and *Famous Bridges and Waterfalls.*

Hiroshige Ando is known for his *Fifty-three Stages of Tokaido.* Tokaido was the road between Edo, the seat of the *Shogun*, and Kyoto, where the Emperor reigned with his court. The Tokaido series included not only scenes along the road but also a great wealth of detail of buildings and people of all classes, often with a bit of humor.

Clay pot with patterns produced by rope. This is a *haniwa* (burial ware) from about A.D. 500.

POTTERY

Painting was not the only graphic art that flourished in Japan. From the early Jomon period (4500–200 B.C.), pottery with surface patterns produced by pressing rope onto wet clay was being made. The potter's wheel came to Japan from Korea with Korean kiln technology in the first three centuries A.D. The Koreans also brought bronze to Japan. Among the early Japanese bronzes were swords and bells which had no practical use. They were objects for magic and rituals, and for burying the dead.

ARCHITECTURE

Japanese architecture is an architecture of wood, a natural material, given the abundance of mountain timber and the need to have light structures to withstand earthquakes. The basic forms came from China but the Japanese developed their own styles.

Traditional houses were wood-framed structures where no attempt was made to hide the structural elements. Paper and rushes were used to fill spaces between panels. The paper and wood frame sliding door was developed: it did not need the space a swinging door required. The wood absorbed some of the summer moisture and released moisture into the air during dry winters. Thatched roofs, 3 feet deep, were popular.

These materials, however, are all combustible, so repositories for valuables, with mud-packed walls, had to be built. Some of Japan's finest structures have burned down and many of the "old" temples are in fact reconstructions of buildings which were razed by fire.

TEMPLES

The oldest structure in Japan is a temple in Nara, the Horyuji, Temple of Noble Law. It was first built in A.D. 607 and rebuilt in 712 after a fire. The Horyuji was the center of arts and scholarship, and its teaching influenced intellectuals throughout Japan. It was founded by Prince Shotoku, who defused the conflict between Shinto and Buddhism; it was from Horyuji that Buddhism spread across Japan. Today the temple houses a huge treasure of priceless objects, including a camphorwood carving of the Buddhist deity Kudara Kannon and the oldest existing embroidery in Japan, called "tapestry of heaven."

The largest wooden structure in the world, also at Nara, is the Great Buddha Hall of the Taodaiji or Great Eastern Temple. The present

The Horyuji of Nara, rebuilt in A.D. 712, is the oldest structure in Japan. The Buddhist images it enshrines are believed to be the originals.

building—161 feet high, 187 feet long and 164 feet wide—was reconstructed in 1708 after the original burned down. It houses the largest bronze statue in the world, a figure of the Great Sun Buddha, which is 71 feet 6 inches high.

Japanese temples are usually groups of several structures: a pagoda, a large hall, sometimes a lecture hall, and quarters for monks and nuns. The pagodas are beautiful structures built to withstand earthquakes. In the great Kanto earthquake of 1923, which destroyed 580,000 houses, the 106-foot, five-storied wooden pagoda at Kaneiji in Ueno Park, Tokyo, survived.

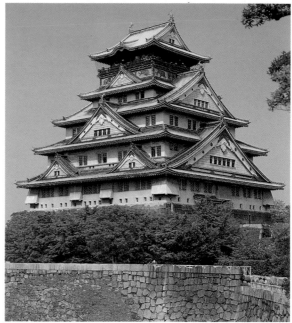

Above: **Himeji Castle (left) and Osaka Castle (right).**

CASTLES

Many Japanese cities were built as castle towns. Castles were built following universal military considerations: a commanding site on high ground or a site protected by water, and maze-like corridors from the entrance to slow down an attacking enemy.

Japanese castles have other special features. They were not built to withstand cannon attack as cannons were rarely used in feudal wars. Only the outer walls were designed for defense, and if these were breached the castle fell to the invader. A castle keep (the innermost stronghold, often a tower) was not designed for a last line of defense as in the case of European castles. Walls were built of stone but the *donjon* (keep) was of timber. Most of the castles standing today have been reconstructed at some time or other.

Japanese castles were built to impress and to symbolize the power of the *daimyo* (chieftains) they housed, as is typical of the Japanese. The façade must inspire fear or admiration; thus, many of their castles are very beautiful.

One of the best known and most beautiful castles in Japan is the Himeji Castle about 20 miles east of Osaka. It was built in 1609 by Terumasa Ikeda, the trusted son-in-law of *Shogun* Ieyasu Tokugawa, as a defense against the western lords. Its towers, with their curving roofs and white walls rising above the heavy gray stone walls, are a magnificent sight. The castle gives the impression of impregnable solidity, yet has elegant and graceful lines. Its other name, White Heron Castle, is apt: it does have the appearance of a great white bird, or a flock of white birds, in flight.

In contrast, about 15 miles east of Himeji Castle, are the ruins of Okayama Castle. Completely black, it is known as the Crow Castle. It was built in 1573, and only two turrets of the original structure remain.

Osaka Castle is steeped in history. This large, majestic structure reflects the ambitions and prestige of *Shogun* Hideyoshi Toyotomi, who built the original castle between 1583 and 1586 with the labor of 630,000 men. Given a strategic position, it was 1.7 miles long and 1.2 miles wide. In 1615 Osaka Castle was besieged and burned by Ieyasu Tokugawa, who took the shogunate from Hideyoshi Toyotomi's son. He ordered that all traces of the old castle be demolished and a new one built on a completely new plan. He wanted to eradicate the symbols left by Hideyoshi Toyotomi and build a castle to stand as a symbol of his power to the lords of the far west.

The new Tokugawa castle was smaller and did not include the outermost moats of the original castle. Fires and a brief civil war in 1867 destroyed it. The present structure is a modern 1931 replica in concrete, which includes some towers built in 1620.

Plan of Himeji Castle, showing:

1	Main citadel
2–5	Citadel
6	Main *donjon* or keep
7	Inner moat
8–18	Gates
19	Water gate 1
20	Water gate 2
21	Gate
22	Moat

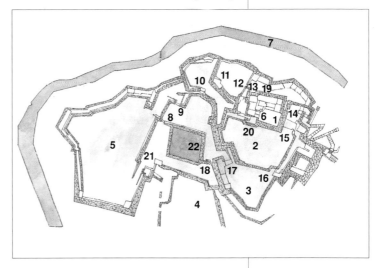

POETRY

Poetry is not the exclusive preserve of intellectuals. Poems appear in newspapers regularly and most Japanese write poems without being abashed about it. It is one of the nation's living arts.

Poetry began as the language of the aristocrats. Emperor Meiji is reputed to have written 100,000 poems. Often, poetry was the only communication between secret lovers. Messengers despatched them with some small symbolic token—a leaf or a fan.

HAIKU Classical Japanese poetry concentrates on distilling a thought in the briefest and most beautiful way. The poet tends to hint and suggest. Here is such a poem by Matsuo Basho (1614–94):

Kare eda ni	On a withered dry branch
karasu no tomarikeru	a crow stops and rests;
aki no kure.	autumn dusk.

The main forms used were called *haiku* (very short poem), *waka* or *tanka* (short poem) and *nagauta* (long poem). The *haiku* was and still is a very popular form. There are strict rules of composition. Basho's poem on the crow is a *haiku*. It is not easy to write *haiku* with its tight line limitations. Nor is *haiku* easy to understand, because there are complex nuances. As in many forms of art, however, constraints bring out some of the finest works.

SENRYU AND ACROSTIC   The *senryu* is a special type of *haiku*. Comical or frivolous, like the limerick, it gave poetry a humorous side.

After he's scolded   Now the man has a child
His wife too much,   He knows all the names
He cooks the rice.   Of the local dogs.

The poets themselves sometimes imposed additional constraints. It showed finesse to send one's lover an acrostic poem, where the first letters of every line spell a word.

*I*n the capital is the one I love, like
*R*obes of stuff so precious, yet now threadbare.
I have come far on this journey,
*S*ad and tearful are my thoughts.
    — from the *Ise Monogatari*

RENGA   The *renga,* or linked poem, was a game, an intellectual challenge. One person wrote two or three lines, the next followed with another two, and so on. Rules controlled not only the syllables; there were patterns to be followed, such as the second verse should mention this or that and the moon should come up in the nth verse, but only once … Practice sharpened the minds and sensitivities of the great poets.

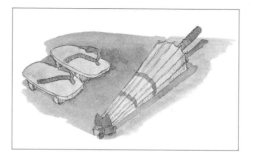

MODERN POETRY

After the Meiji Restoration the influences of European free verse caused major changes in poetic forms. A nation of highly disciplined poets showed that in spite of the confines of their past, individuality could break through. Here are two examples:

My nails are cut
My manicure is done
My blouse is ironed
My shoes are polished
And now,
I only go to your funeral.
— Takata Kyoko

Going into the room,
You hesitate, standing for a while.
It's lemon.
You notice.
There's pain.

Eventually you find the wound.

This is the frightening thing;
that in every part of time, there's a delay.
— Kitamura Taro

HISTORICAL NOVELS

Classical Japanese prose began in the Heian period (A.D. 794–1185), and was mainly the work of women. Relegated to a lowly position, they found expression in writing. This period also saw the development of the *kana* scripts, which opened the way to easier writing. Major works produced then included *Tosa Diary, Taketori Tales, Tales of Ise, Utsubo Tales* and the two classics, *Tales of Genji* and *Pillow Book*.

Tales of Genji, written about A.D. 1000 by Lady Murasaki Shikibu, is perhaps the Heian work with the greatest influence on Japanese literature. Generations of Japanese scholars have read and dissected this tale of fiction woven around Lady Murasaki's realistic and minute observations of court life. It was a new kind of novel, having nothing dramatic, unnatural or improbable in it. The style is ornate and indirect.

The *Pillow Book*, or *Pillow Sketches*, of Sei Shonagon is another outstanding work by a Japanese woman. It introduced an open and easy style and revealed the author's opinions and feelings. The book's postscript is typical of her style.

> It has become too dark for literary work, and my pen is worn out. I will bring these sketches to a close. They are a record of that which I have seen with my eyes and felt with my heart, not written that others might read them, but put together to solace the loneliness of my home life. When I think how I tried to keep them secret, conscious of vulgar and exaggerated remarks which have escaped me, the tears flow uncontrollably.

A section of the *Tales of Genji* picture scroll, which is considered a masterpiece in its own right. It is believed to have been produced in the early 12th century.

DECLINE AND REVIVAL OF LITERATURE

Towards the end of Heian, and in the Kamakura period that followed, several major written works dealt with historical subjects: *Yeigwa Monogatari, O-Kagami, Gempei Seisuiki, Heiki Monogatari* (*monogatari* means "tale" or "narrative").

Japanese literature declined in the Kamakura period and thereafter, reaching its lowest point by the end of the Muromachi period. Intellectuals turned to China, as is reflected in the literature and social codes. Women were thrust out of public life in conformity with Chinese thinking.

The Tokugawa period (1603–1867) saw great changes in the literary scene. The printing press had been established, script and grammar simplified and vocabulary expanded. Writers began to address not only the aristocrats but also the common people. There was a new Japaneseness breaking away from Chinese cultural

Sora bidding farewell to Basho.

millstones, although a great many Chinese words were absorbed at this time. It was then that the great *haiku* poets, including Basho, wrote their masterpieces.

Among the outstanding writers of the Tokugawa period are Saikaku Ibara (1642–93) with his new style of realism and humor reminiscent of *Tales of Genji* and *Pillow Book*; Bakin Kiokutei (1767–1848), who wrote what is perhaps the most famous novel after *Tales of Genji*, the *Hakkuden*; and Ikku Jipensha (?–1831), author of one of the most humorous of novels, *Hizakurige*, which has been compared to *The Pickwick Papers*.

MODERN LITERATURE

After the Meiji Restoration when Japan set out to catch up with two hundred years of western development, there was an explosion of fiction writing. It was a vigorous growth both in terms of volume and a blossoming of Japan's finest writers.

The Japanese read voraciously, not just for knowledge but mainly for pleasure. Today Japan has the highest ratio of novels printed per capita in the world. There is a large book market for popular romances and thrillers, as well as historical novels.

Modern Japanese writers explore styles and themes quite different from those of past novels. They have become greatly absorbed in the psychology of the characters; in this, they resemble western writers. Yet there is a special Japanese slant, always present, reflecting the Japanese mind today, a mixture of tradition and individuality.

Women novelists have always held a significant position in Japanese fiction. Enchi Fumiko, born in 1895, is in a class of her own among modern women writers. Her books span the major changing era in Japanese literature. Conscious of the suppression of Japanese women over the last 600 years, she has written many stories on that theme. *Onnazaka* (*The Waiting Years* is the English title) took her eight years to complete and won a top prize in the Japanese literary world.

Yasunari Kawabata (1899–1972) was the only Japanese awarded the Nobel Prize, in 1965, for his novelettes, *Snow Country* and *Thousand Cranes*. Yukio Mishima (1925–70), one of the best known in the west today, was an intellectual of very strong opinions whose books do not represent modern Japanese writing. His novels deal with the more sordid aspects of life, but his contribution to world literature is undeniable. He killed himself by committing *seppuku* in public in 1970.

Soseki Natsume, one of the first post-Restoration writers (1867–1916) educated in the west. His best known books are *Botchan*, *I am a Cat* and *The Heart of Things*. His portrait figures on a Japanese banknote.

"The art of allusion, or this love of allusion in art, is at the root of the noh."

— *Ezra Pound, a scholar and interpreter of noh*

JAPANESE THEATER

Japanese theater, which is always intertwined with dance and music, began in the 7th century A.D. with the Shinto ritualistic dances. These dances are still performed today in essentially the same form. The *noh* drama which developed in the 14th century is one of the main branches of Japanese theater.

NOH   *Noh* plays are a mixture of dance and drama based on Shinto dances and Buddhist teachings. The subject matter includes the sin of killing, the after-life, the transience of this world, the power of Buddha and the evil of lust. In spite of the seriousness underlying the themes, costumes are colorful, elaborately embroidered and brocaded with silver and gold.

The action on stage is in the form of "flashbacks" from the memories of the characters. They are obscure, idyllic and lyrical and the script is heavy with allusion and symbolism. The dialogue—archaic phrases in chanted tones—is incomprehensible to present-day audiences, and even educated Japanese need a script to follow the play.

Noh started as an amusement performed in temple grounds for the people, but the aristocracy adopted it as their private theater and in the Tokugawa period legally deprived the people of *noh*. Only warriors were allowed to witness *noh*, although, because of its Buddhist influence, *noh* seldom included warrior roles.

Noh reached its peak in the 15th century, decayed and was revived in the early 20th century. A traditional *noh* theater program would include five *noh* plays with three or four *kyogen* plays in between.

KYOGEN *Kyogen* is a comic interlude. The word means "mad words" and, as in *noh*, the performers are all men. *Kyogen* reveals many different and significant facets of Japanese character.

Kyogen plays were originally performed in temples to relieve the strain of prolonged Buddhist services. They are short, very humorous and never involve more than three characters. About a third of the themes are of a servant mocking his feudal lord. The lord is invariably made to look ridiculous but is eventually proven right. In the past, common people and lords enjoyed these skits. Another third or so of *kyogen* themes poke fun at Buddhism, even though Buddhism was then the religion of the aristocracy and it was in Buddhist temples that *kyogen* was performed.

The costumes of *kyogen* are those of the 15th century but the language is the language of the 17th century: *kyogen*, unlike *noh*, was passed down from generation to generation orally and only written down in the 17th century.

A temple attendant performs a ritual dance in a Shinto temple. Japanese theater, in fact, began in the grounds of these temples and the dances performed on stage today have not changed much from the original forms.

KABUKI The three characters that make up *kabuki* mean song, dance and skill. In its heyday, *kabuki* attracted thousands. *Kabuki* flowered in the Genroku period (1673–1735) when great novelists and poets like Basho were bringing a new impetus to the arts. Japan's greatest playwright, Monzaemon Chikamatsu (1653–1725), was in his prime, and the first of a dynasty of actors started: the Danjuro line. *Kabuki* reached its peak in the 18th century.

Kabuki is melodramatic and spectacular. Climaxes require a special look called the *mie*; to the accompaniment of wooden clappers, the actor strikes a grandiose pose, widening eyes and crossing one of them. Unlike *noh,* which always has the same backdrop of a pine tree painting, *kabuki* has elaborate props like trapdoors and a revolving stage. A close rapport exists between actors and audience, aided by a walkway that extends into the audience. Actors address some lines to the audience, members of which shout their comments as the play progresses.

Kabuki plots revolve around the elevation of a commoner to a higher status, people changing forms, women changing into men, incredible swordfights, lovers' suicide pacts and a terrible Japanese insult—slapping someone with a slipper or clog.

BUNRAKU *Bunraku*, the puppet theater, developed from storytelling into a musical form in the 16th century. Storytelling is still very popular in Japan: every television station devotes at least an hour a day to the traditional half-recited, half-sung style of storytelling.

Today, puppets are mechanically complicated things about 3 feet high. To operate one puppet requires three men. The puppeteers are not hidden, but as soon as the play begins the audience ceases to notice the puppeteers.

MUSIC

Japanese music, like many aspects of the theatrical arts, has Chinese origins. The Chinese three-stringed fiddle, in particular, made a major change with its new sounds, which are quite different to those produced by the Japanese lute. Music is inextricably linked with dance and, through dance, the theater.

With the opening of Japan to the rest of the world, the Japanese absorbed all forms of western music with great fervor and no cultural conflicts whatsoever. Traditional Japanese music ceased to develop from about the 18th century.

Bunraku or puppet theater. The puppet is manipulated by a few men who are not hidden.

LEISURE

SPORTS CRAZE

WITH THE internationalizing of leisure via television and recorded music, Japanese leisure styles are similar to those in North America and Europe. They have absorbed pop music and adopted baseball with as widespread and intense an enthusiasm as one sees in America. Golf is the hobby of the upper class; tennis and skiing are the craze of the masses.

The sports craze is not wholly due to pleasure-seeking. It has become a necessity because, along with other things, many Japanese have adopted a western diet. Once on a low-calorie diet of *tofu*, seafood and *miso* soup, many are now eating fattening amounts of meat and junk food.

A new feature of cities such as Tokyo is the indoor sports club. To cater to several sports interests, and because of space constraints, such clubs are housed in multi-story buildings. Thus, for membership fees varying from as little as 50,000 yen ($350) to as much as 700,000 yen ($5,000), and a nominal entrance fee, the Japanese can swim, play indoor baseball, racquet games, work out in aerobics classes or in a gymnasium, and even play a round of golf! Then, after the exercise, go for a sauna, and of course a snack—all under one roof.

Opposite: **Shopping, anywhere in the world, is a favorite pastime and Japan is no exception. The stores are well stocked with designer items and crafts.**

Below: **Nearly all universities and high schools in Japan have their own team. Baseball programs are top-rated on TV and some American players play on Japanese teams. The game was first played in 1873; Japan's annual series started in 1903.**

TRAVEL, READING AND PACHINKO

Japanese travel a lot, but mostly in organized groups. They have a passion for photography: whether abroad or at home, the Japanese photograph almost anything they see.

Reading newspapers, magazines or novels is a passion. Comics (*manga*) have become a craze in recent years, and range from pornographic to Shakespeare's plays, from funny to serious. Japanese seem to read them everywhere. Restaurants provide stacks of *manga* for their customers and truck drivers keep a *manga* on the seat beside them.

At night the night spots and bars of Japan ring with the same guffaws as they do all over the world. Japanese drink regularly, although many westerners believe that their capacity to hold liquor is low.

One of their more unusual leisure pursuits is *pachinko*, the pinball machine. In the cities, thousands of businessmen and workers stand side by side, pushing the lever to set the balls moving, apparently oblivious to their surroundings. *Pachinko* is a mindless activity and the prizes are insignificant. Yet, it has been reported that 15 million people, mostly men, spend more than US$3 billion a year on this game, which they play daily, in many cases for hours on end. It is a form of escapism, like their drinking bars and their comics.

There are still traditional Japanese facets to their leisure. The appreciation of the old is alive and strong in the Japanese. They travel around Japan to see the old temples, castles, rock gardens and the famous scenic spots. It is not just aesthetic appreciation; there is a nationalistic pride in all this.

In a nation which has the highest per capita GNP in the world, relatively simple housing and without an attitude of ostentatious consumption equal to that of the west, the amount spent on leisure activities is high.

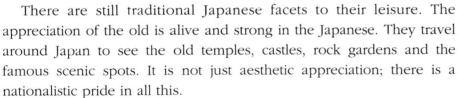

Japan's troubled past gave rise to a warrior class, skilled in the art of weaponry and arm-to-arm combat. Modern sports derived from ancient arts of warfare have taken away none of the skill, flexibility, speed or tenacity of combat, but they have added rules for judging tournaments in judo (top), *kendo* or fencing (center) and sumo wrestling (bottom).

THE JAPANESE BATH

Bathing is a very important daily activity to the Japanese. The word "bath" —*O-furo*—is given the honorable prefix *O*.

The Japanese have no qualms about showing their naked bodies. Public baths in the country are still places where men and women bathe together. They start by washing every part of the body meticulously, often asking a friend or acquaintance to scrub their backs. Having made sure that they are clean, they get into the bath-pool or bathtub and sit in it, soaking in the heat of very hot water for a long time.

FESTIVALS

FESTIVALS (*matsuri*) are major social events in Japan. Whether religious, superstitious, or rooted in ancient events now irrelevant, they allow the disciplined Japanese to relax and let their hair down.

NEW YEAR FESTIVAL

New Year's Day, January 1, is celebrated by the family, the public and businesses. Three bamboo and pine branches are put up in front of the house and a rope stretched across the gate. In the lounge, decorative rice cakes, seaweed, dried sardines and persimmons, and a lobster with evergreens or ferns, are placed on a special stand. *Zoni*, a soup of pounded rice cakes, vegetables and fish or chicken, is eaten. *Toso*, a special spiced *sake*, is drunk and a stack of trays called the "heavy boxes" is packed with tidbits for visitors.

It is a day for visiting the local shrine and for calling on one's friends and relatives; these days, it could be a day to sit in front of the TV set because excellent traditional programs are broadcast on New Year's Day.

January 2 in many ways is regarded as the first day of the year. One does one's first calligraphy, writes the first poem, plays the first musical piece, sews the first stitches, and gathers sentimental treasures around the pillow to ensure the first dream of the year is happy. Tradesmen used to decorate carts gaily before setting out on the first business day.

The festival ends on January 7, when a rice porridge seasoned with seven herbal grasses is eaten. Traditional events, such as the reading of poems at the Emperor's Poetry Party on January 18, drag the festivities on a little longer.

Opposite: **Gion originated in Kyoto, but it is now celebrated elsewhere in Japan. Here, men in costume carry a float through Narita.**

Below: **In rabbit wrap and gay *kimono*, a young girl sets out to celebrate New Year's Day.**

TANABATA

The Tanabata festival arises out of a Chinese story of romance and symbolism. Tanabata-tsume, a weaver girl-star, fell in love with a cowherd and in the whirlwind of a honeymoon they neglected their duties. The god of the firmament separated them. On the seventh night of the seventh month magpies form a bridge across the celestial river dividing them, but the lovers can only cross if it does not rain, and the river is narrow enough.

On July 7, this romance is symbolized by two bamboo cuttings set up in each house, one representing the male and the other the female. They are decorated with poems on strips of different-colored paper, and are later dropped into a river. At Sendai thousands of folk dancers in light summer *kimono* and flower-decorated straw hats dance through the town after dark.

BON

The purpose of the Bon, or O-Bon, festival originally was to offer prayers and do ritual dances in the Buddhist month when ghosts of the dead were believed to return to earth. From this 14th century custom it has become a summer festival of dancing and lanterns.

Candles and floating lanterns on rivers and lakes (supplemented by fireworks these days) guide the spirits back to the paradise or hell they came from. In temples and graveyards flickering lights bring an air of quiet eeriness and subdued festivity.

In the village squares, towers are set up where drummers, and perhaps a band, pound out an all-night rhythm, pacing the feet and hand movements of hundreds of ordinary folk dancing in concentric circles around the towers, repeating the same simple movements for hours on end, rapt in a trance.

In China's remote past, dolls were part of the ritual cleansing of ill fortune. Paper dolls were made and given the owner's bad luck, then cast into rivers or lakes. Japan's Hinamatsuri may have begun for the same reason, but the dolls today are far too valuable to throw away.

HINAMATSURI

This dolls' festival is really "girls' day" in Japan, the only day when girls get to play with beautiful dolls, works of fine craftsmanship. The family's treasured doll collection is brought out and displayed on tiered shelves for about two weeks. There are usually more than ten dolls; the emperor and empress dolls are put on the top

step. The doll display is often accompanied by an equally exquisite display of miniature furniture and food.

A special sweet and mild *sake* is drunk and the girls of the family play hostess to the boys and friends who visit them to admire the dolls. Hinamatsuri is their day.

Above: Costume and pageantry—sometimes bizarre, always colorful—mark the Toshogu Shrine Grand Festival.

Opposite: Carried, pushed, or, in this case, pulled, the floats make their way through the main streets during Gion.

TOSHOGU SHRINE GRAND FESTIVAL

This is a Shinto religious extravaganza. Yet it is said to commemorate the death of Ieyasu Tokugawa, one of the three warlords who molded Japan into a single homogeneous country. Three movable shrines are carried around to various other shrines in the Toshogu shrine complex, in a pageant of a thousand marchers in Tokugawa period costumes, accompanied by a motley crowd of followers dressed as monkeys, lions, *samurai*, falconers, fairies, etc.

There is something for everyone: religious shrine dances, other special dances performed by Buddhist priests, and even a demonstration of mounted archery.

DAIMONJI BONFIRE

Every year, as the O-Bon celebrations of the month of ghosts culminate in a night of bonfires and lanterns all over Japan, residents of Kyoto and the surrounding district settle down to watch Mount Nyoigatake. At 8:00 p.m. on August 16, a bonfire starts burning and slowly spreads out to form the character *dai* (big) on the mountain slope. *Dai* resembles a man with arms and legs stretched out. The bonfires cover an area of about 12,000 square yards. *Daimonji* means "a large character fire."

Soon fires start burning on other hills, each in the form of the character, *dai*. It is a spectacular finale to the month of festivities for visiting ghosts from other worlds.

GION MATSURI OF KYOTO

On July 17 the ancient and dignified city of Kyoto, with its beautiful temples and serene parks and gardens of mosses and rock, erupts into a brilliant spectacle. The Gion Matsuri brings color and music, gaiety and open friendliness. From 9:00 to 11:00 a.m., a procession of 29 carved or gilded floats, decorated with tapestries, gongs, flutes and drums, are carried or drawn through the town. Old family houses and old stores throw open their doors, displaying their treasures and family heirlooms.

Everyone is spontaneous and out to enjoy themselves. There is an almost Latin fiesta atmosphere, making it difficult to reconcile the Gion festival with its origin in A.D. 876, when the people of Kyoto prayed for divine protection against an epidemic, which was sweeping across the country.

The carp, symbol of courage and endurance, make attractive streamers on Boys' Day.

BOYS' DAY FESTIVAL

On the fifth day of the fifth month Japanese boys have their day. Mounted on poles at almost every house, brightly colored carp-shaped banners of paper or cloth flutter in the wind like flags or runway air-socks. Five hundred years ago these were first put up to frighten away the swarms of May insects.

A tiered stand in every house displays the family collection of warrior figures and instruments of war: perhaps an antique family sword, a silk banner of the family crest or a set of spears. Nowadays May 5 is also celebrated as Children's Day, but the older tradition lingers, of wishing the boys of the family health and the courage and fortitude of *samurai*.

THE KUROFUNE MATSURI OF SHIMODA

The Japanese celebrate Commodore Perry's landing at Shimoda on the Izu peninsula. *Kuro* means "black" and *fune* means "ship." Kurofune Matsuri is the Black Ship festival. The blackness of the tarred hulls of U.S. naval ships made a menacing impression on the Japanese because they never painted the hulls of their boats. In spite of the unwelcome intrusion in 1857, the Kurofune festival commemorates the event with a historical pageant every year around May 17. There is also a U.S. naval parade.

AOI MATSURI

The Aoi Matsuri is reputed to be the oldest festival celebrated in the world. From the 6th century A.D. the pageant of color and costumes, with its accompaniment of music from flutes, gongs and drums, has snaked its way through the streets of Kyoto. The Hollyhock festival, as it is sometimes known, is celebrated on May 15, between the last of the cherry blossoms and the first irises.

The highlight is the Imperial procession, re-enacted these days in the dress of the Heian (9th to 12th century) period with the Imperial ox-cart, its lacquer beautifully preserved and its wheels squeaking to attest to its authenticity. Brocaded *kimono* with huge sleeves, sprays of artificial wisteria, funny little black hats perched on top of the attendants' heads, ornate saddles and enormously impractical umbrellas decorated with flowers and a seemingly endless array of strange and colorful costumes all add up to make the Aoi festival a dazzling spectacle.

The Imperial ox-cart brought out for the Aoi festival Kyoto became the capital of Japan in the 8th century.

The kite battle of the Hamamatsu festival is held over three days, and the entire city turns up for the event. Each kite bears a neighborhood's insignia, and the object of the fight is to bring down kites belonging to other neighborhoods.

HAMAMATSU MATSURI

The Suwa shrine festival at Hamamatsu in Shizuoka is not just another shrine festival. It includes the *Hamamatsu Odakoage*: the big-kite fight at Nakatajima beach. It began about 1550, when a feudal lord announced the name of his newborn son by flying a large kite with the child's name on it.

Today up to 60 teams from different districts manipulate giant kites with unbelievable agility, skill and intense excitement, trying to cut each other's kite string with the abrasive strings of their own kites. It is a tumult of shouting, leaping, jostling, laughing—a riot of color and splendor with all the tension of a football final and the gaiety of an outdoor springtime party.

HAKONE TORII MATSURI

This is the festival for travelers celebrated by the lake of Ashinoko (also known as Lake Ashi and Lake Hakone), in the mountains south of Tokyo.

The Torii Matsuri originated from casting little paper replicas of *torii* (gateway structures) into the lake to ensure safety when traveling. It has been blown up today to a glittering spectacle by burning a life-size *torii,* afloat on the lake, which is decorated with one thousand lanterns.

TENJIN MATSURI OF OSAKA

The Tenjin Matsuri of Osaka is one of the greatest and most dazzling of the festivals of Japan. It began when the people of Osaka brought pieces of paper cut out in human forms, as offerings against the diseases that spread in the summer heat, to Temmangu shrine. These paper offerings were then carried down to the river and thrown into the water.

Today the festival is centered around a magnificent procession which starts on land from Temmangu shrine and moves down to floats drifting on the river between bonfires on the banks as night falls. The procession begins as six frenzied men beat on a 5-foot diameter drum as if possessed, and is followed by a scarlet-robed horseman, dancers with spinning umbrellas, an ox-cart bearing books, boxes of rice offerings, palanquins, portable shrines, a lion dance and, to ensure that dozens of proud parents will share the joy of the day, streams of powdered, rouged and prettied-up children.

SHIRAOI-NO-IOMANTE

This is a solemn hunting festival of the Ainu, the aboriginal people of Japan who now live only in Hokkaido. The Iomante, or bear festival, originated from the sacrificial killing of a baby bear especially reared for the annual event. It was believed that the spirit of the bear went up to heaven.

The baby bear is not sacrificed anymore but a hideous, grotesque thing, almost like a face from a science fiction fantasy, represents the bear.

BUDDHA'S BIRTHDAY

Buddha's birthday is celebrated in Buddhist temples all over Japan with the *Kamabutsu* ceremony, the baptizing of Buddha. It was first performed at the Genkoji temple, Yamato in A.D. 606.

In the temple grounds, an image of the infant Buddha is set up under a roof decorated with flowers; this is the *hanamido*, temple of flowers. The priests give worshipers a sweet tea made from hydrangea leaves to take home.

Buddha's birthday has thus come to be associated with flowers, and in Hibaya Park, Tokyo, thousands of flower-bearing Buddhist children march in procession.

NAMAHAGE

Namahage is celebrated at the Akagami shrine of Oga city, Akita. It is a strange mixture of a harvest festival and an orgy of scaring children into obedience throughout the year ahead.

After prayers in front of a bonfire, young unmarried men dressed in straw cloaks and trousers, with frightening masks and bells around their waists, sometimes carrying a wooden pail and a wooden replica of a kitchen knife, go from house to house, knocking on the doors and asking "Is there any wicked person in this house?" They are invited in and offered rice cakes and *sake*, and move on, chuckling and getting more and more drunk.

It is fun for the young men but a nightmare for the little ones.

"Wo–! Wo–! Are there any bad children here? Any crying children?"

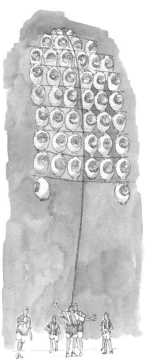

Right: **The flower hat dance of the Hanagasa festival.**

Below: **A competitor in a festival contest.**

HANAGASA-ODORI

This is one of the great festivals of Tohoku, celebrated at Yamagata on August 6 and 8. The *hanagasa* is a hat on which flowers are painted.

The *Hanagasa* dance swamps one by the sheer numbers—thousands of girls, swinging their hats from above their heads to almost down to their knees in circles in a steady rhythm to the music, crying out, thousands of voices in unison, "*Yassho! Makasho! Yassho! Makasho!*"

DEER-DANCE FESTIVAL

This is a delightful fall festival of Ehime province. Young boys dressed in tubular armless robes with deer-head masks, complete with antlers, beat small drums as they step and sway in a graceful dance, searching for the "doe" hiding from them. At the Awatsuhiko shrine, Awajima, Ehime, a very special eight-deer dance, the *Yatsushishi-odori*, is particularly well known. (*Odori* means "dance.")

Deer dances, *Shishi-odori*, have been performed at fall festivals in Ehime since the 17th century.

CALENDAR OF JAPANESE FESTIVALS*

New Year	Jan 3, 6 & 7	Pan-Japan	
Iwate Snow festival	Feb 3–12	Tohoku	Ice sculptures
Hinamatsuri	Mar 3	Pan-Japan	Dolls
Kasuga Matsuri	Mar 13	Nara	Lanterns
Buddha's Birthday	Apr 8		Buddha procession
Osaka Int'l festival of music	Apr 14–May 2	Osaka	Includes classical Japanese theater
Fire-walking	Apr 15	Miyajima	Includes *Bugaku*, an ancient dance of Central Asia, seen only in Japan
Hamamatsu festival	May 3–5	Shizuoka	Big-kite fights
Boys' Day	May 5	Pan-Japan	Carp streamers
Aoi Matsuri (Hollyhock festival)	May 15	Simogano, Kamigamo	Imperial procession, flower decorated umbrellas
Toshogu Shrine Grand Festival	May 17–18	Nikko	Tokugawa period pageant, archery
Takigi-Noh	Jun 1–3	Kyoto	
Gion Matsuri	Jul 16–17	Kyoto	Floats
Nomaoi	Jul 23–24	Tohoku	Wild horse chasing
Bon	Jul 13–17 Aug 8–24	Pan-Japan Kyoto	Floating lanterns, fireworks
Black Ship festival, Kurofune Matsuri	Jul 14 May 17	Kurihama Shimoda	Historical pageant
Tanabata (Star festival)	Aug 6–8	Sendai	Bamboo branches with colored paper ornaments and love poems
Hanagasa-odori	Aug 7–9	Yamagata	
Bonbori Matsuri	Aug 7–9	Kamakura	Lanterns
Daimonji bonfire	Aug 16	Kyoto	Bonfires in character "Dai"
Kokeshi festival	Sep 7–9	Miyagi	Costume parade, dances, memorial service for imperfect dolls destroyed the year before
Iomante, Ainu Bear Festival	Oct 22	Hokkaido	
Tenjin Matsuri		Osaka	Procession—land and river
Emperor's Birthday	Dec 23		

Dates in 1989

FOOD AND DRINK

JAPANESE food does not fall into the generalization of "Asian" food. In tastes and above all in presentation it reflects the character and culture of the Japanese. It is a low-protein diet based on rice and, to a lesser degree, noodles. The main sources of protein are fish and soy beans. The flavorings are generally subtle, with sugar and soy sauce their main ingredients.

Food is always presented to please the eye and whet the appetite. It has been said that the Japanese "eat with their eyes." They were using different shaped dishes long before the west broke from their rigid limitation of round plates. They have many rules on presentation: one such rule is that a whole fish is always placed before the guest with its head to his right.

STAPLES

Though rice is the main carbohydrate, noodles are often eaten. The range of noodle dishes varies from the thick *udon* to the very fine *soba* noodles. *Soba* is sometimes eaten cold, dipped in a sweet soy sauce with finely chopped scallions floating in it. In a unique food-and-fun festival event, soupy noodles are poured down a bamboo trough alongside which hungry eaters use chopsticks to gobble and suck in the noodles as they flow past.

A popular and unusual tuber carbohydrate is *konyakku*. It is believed to have come from Indonesia and now grows in a limited area in Japan. *Konyakku* is eaten raw, boiled or reconstituted from *konyakku* flour. Though highly priced, it is relished.

Yam, which the Japanese call "mountain potato," is another favorite. Fried in batter or steamed, the yam appears frequently.

FISH IS THEIR FORTE ...

...Fish grilled on a steel plate called a *teppan*, fish boiled in soy sauce, fish cakes and fish balls. Dried and fermented *bonito* (*katsuo-bushi*) is used in their *miso* (soybean paste) soup and shavings of it are used for garnishing. A favorite flavoring is a thick sauce made from boiled fish.

The Japanese love raw fish, *sashimi*, an expensive delicacy eaten as a starter with *wasabi*, a Japanese mustard, and thin slices of ginger. It is more common in *sushi*, little pieces of raw fish on one-mouthful lumps of vinegared rice, eaten as a snack or a tidbit to go with drinks.

The origin of *sushi* is interesting. Transportation of fresh sea fish inland was slow, and a sour, fermented rice and fish mixture was eaten to mask the decaying fish smell. When fermentation was discontinued, vinegar was added to maintain the essential flavor. Now only the freshest fish is used.

FISH BELIEFS Most Japanese remember some form of fish calender: when to eat salmon, trout, tuna, etc. The first *bonito* of the season is highly rated. The Japanese have many "fish" theories: one concerns the *sanma*, a fish not widely eaten elsewhere, which is supposed to cure various ills. It is said "when the *sanma* comes, the masseurs go away."

Fish is also often found in their poetry and comic verse. It appears in various emblems, such as the carp-shaped banners put up on the boys' festival day.

OTHER SEAFOOD Japanese eat other seafood, including seaweed. Seaweed is a major source of minerals and other trace elements, such as iodine, in their diet. Eels are a specialty. *Kabayaki* (grilled eel) is a mouthwatering dish. The eel is steamed first and then grilled dark brown and placed on top of a bowl of rice.

An interesting prawn was discovered by accident when a fisherman made a mistake in lowering his nets and drew up a pinkish, transparent prawn never before seen. The Japanese call it the *sakura* (cherry blossom) prawn because of its color.

SUSHI

Sushi is not restricted to raw fish. Hundreds of variants have different tidbits to go with the rice, including cucumber, cooked egg, steamed prawns, raw cuttlefish, seaweed and shellfish.

Sushi is presented in bite-sized pieces. One takes up a piece, turns it around, dips the topping in a saucer of soy sauce with pungent *wasabi*, and puts the whole morsel into one's mouth. This is a little tricky at first.

PORK, BEEF AND VENISON

Pork came to Kyushu from China, via Korea, and the best pork dishes are thus found in the south. They have their pork chops (*tonkatsu*) and other dishes, but in general pork has not developed into a major food item in Japan.

The window display is the menu. Plastic dishes of items on the menu, with prices in some cases, help customers decide what to eat or what suits their budget before entering the restaurant.

Japanese eat beef only as special dishes. *Sukiyaki*, thin strips of meat cooked with vegetables in front of diners, is one such dish. They have developed *kobe* beef for their particular preferences. Cattle are fattened and massaged so that fat is dispersed in the muscle and appears in the cooked meat as finely dispersed globules. *Kobe* beef is probably the most expensive beef in the world.

Venison is one of Japan's more unusual meats. The best venison is believed to come from Hokkaido, where the deer supposedly eat grasses with medicinal properties. The Japanese also eat horsemeat. Like the Germans and French, Japanese enjoy the uncommon taste and texture of horsemeat. It is sometimes eaten raw as *sashimi*.

VEGETABLES

Japanese vegetables embrace those well known in Europe and Asia and include leafy vegetables such as spinach, fruit vegetables like aubergines, flowers, stems and roots. There are many not familiar to the western world, such as *fuki* (butter-burr), burdock, *daikon* (a kind of radish) and even chrysanthemum leaves. *Daikon*, especially thinly sliced, is seen in most Japanese meals as an individual dish, a pickle or garnish.

EGGS

The Japanese have their own ways of handling eggs. *Chawan-mushi* (literally "steamed in a cup") are steamed whipped eggs with tasty additions. In cities the *okonomiya* (omelette shops) provide the customer with a staggering choice of omelettes.

TOFU

When Buddhism discouraged meat it popularized the soy bean, a vegetable protein. *Tofu*, the soybean cake, is ubiquitous in Japan. Cold and hot, as drink and food, as vegetable and sweet—Japanese food would not be the same without it.

Making soybean cake became an art. Buddhist temples vied with each other in the development of the perfect soybean cake, and out of this came Japanese "silken *tofu*." An unusual dish offered in restaurants is the "soybean steak," a fried soybean cake with a thick, sweet soy sauce topped with dried fish shavings.

Vegetable vendors materialize magically during festivals. These flimsy structures are obviously temporary and are located near temple grounds. Spiritual and practical concerns are thus dealt with conveniently.

FROM SHABU-SHABU TO SAKE

SHABU-SHABU AND SOY-SAUCE STEWS   The universal stew, so welcome when one comes in from the winter cold, is also found in Japan. Many Japanese stews are flavored with soy sauce. They call these stews *nimono*. There are hundreds, all as delicious as Chinese claypots and French coq-au-vin. There is also the Japanese version of the fondue and "steamboat," called *shabu-shabu*, a word without literal meaning which conveys the sound of bubbling soup in which one dips and cooks a selection of raw meats and vegetables.

TEMPURA   *Tempura* is prawns, fish, aubergine, etc. deep-fried after being dipped in a special batter. The Japanese learned it from the Portuguese and incorporated into their food vocabulary the Portuguese word *tempora* (temporary thing). The Roman Catholic Portuguese could not eat meat on Fridays, so they called the fish-fried-in-batter dish a "temporary thing."

PICKLES AND HERBS   Japanese food tastes are generally subtle, so they provide sharp stimulants in a dazzling variety of pickles (*tsukemono*). Pickled radish and cucumber—crisp, biting, different, just a little pungent and sour—add the finishing touch to the Japanese meal.

Even their herbs and spicy tubers are sensitive but subtle, and play an important role in Japanese cuisine.

SWEETS   Japanese have crystallized fruit and spun sugar like the English floss, but not the Chinese range of hot sweets. Soy beans form the base of many Japanese sweets. The best flour dumplings are ones with a sweet soybean center.

Their presentation is unique in shapes and forms, and particularly in the packaging. It is one more example of the visual art which permeates the whole fabric of Japanese society.

The Japanese tea-drinking ceremony is performed according to rituals and rules that demand full participation from the host and guests. In the 16th century, Japan's most famous tea master, Sen no Rikyu, insisted that only humble natural materials such as bamboo be used. Pottery made in Japan was included, and China tea was relegated to the background.

Today, traditional establishments are being overtaken by the *kissaten*, places serving non-alcoholic drinks—tea, coffee, cocoa, chocolate, milk shakes, floats, together with light snacks like cake and sandwiches.

Opposite: **Barrels of *sake* (bottom) and a *sake* establishment (top) run by the local authorities. *Sake* or Japanese rice wine was first made in and for the Imperial court. The basis is yeast made from rice, malted rice and water. Drinking *sake* while contemplating nature's beauty is a traditional pastime.**

TEA AND *SAKE* Tea is the drink of Japan. It appears in front of a visitor and at all meals. The Japanese use the honorific *O* in front of the word "tea" and always refer to tea as *O-cha*. The living room of a house is called the *cha-no-ma*, literally the tea room. Many hundred years ago they developed a formal ceremony for the preparation and offering of tea to special guests which is today regarded as an art form.

Sake is the main Japanese alcoholic drink. It is made from rice wine and is usually drunk warmed, though a few rare *sake* are traditionally drunk chilled. Today cold *sake* is something of a new fad. A sweetened *sake*, *mirin*, is used for cooking. Special varieties include *amazake*, a sweet *sake*, and another with the fin of the puffer fish (blowfish) in it.

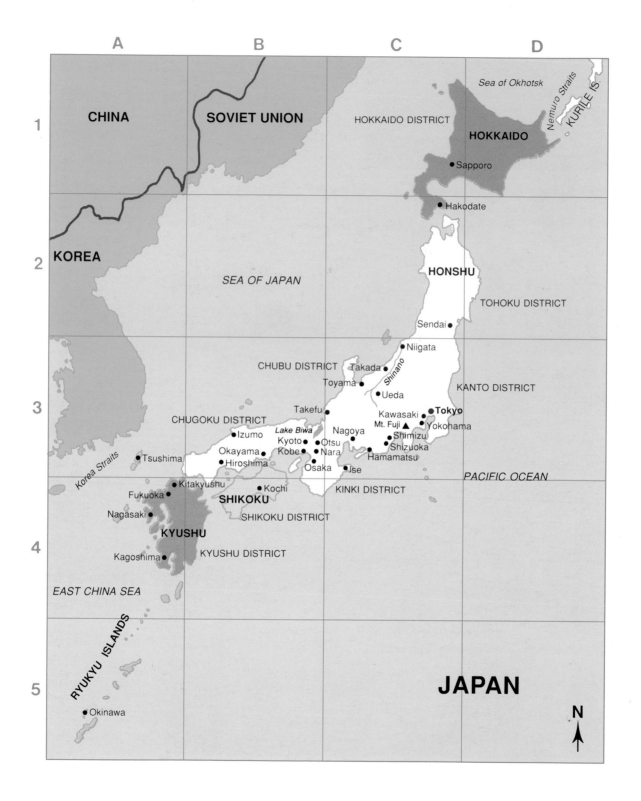

JAPAN

International Boundary
▲   Mountain
●   Capital
●   City
〰   River
🔻   Lake

QUICK NOTES

LAND AREA
145,830 square miles

POPULATION
122.7 million

CAPITAL
Tokyo

NATIONAL ANTHEM
Kimigayo ("The Reign of Our Emperor")

MAJOR ISLANDS
Hokkaido, Honshu, Shikoku, Kyushu

MAJOR RIVER
The Shinano

MAJOR LAKE
Lake Biwa

HIGHEST POINT
Mt. Fuji (12,389 feet)

CLIMATE
Temperate, with four seasons. Heaviest rainfall
is from June to July.

NATIONAL LANGUAGE
Japanese

MAJOR RELIGIONS
Buddhism, Shinto

CURRENCY
Yen
(US$1 = 146 yen)

MAIN EXPORTS
Vehicles, iron and steel, scientific instruments,
telecommunication and electronic equipment,
chemicals, office equipment, ships, and
textiles.

JAPANESE ERAS

Nara	710–794
Heian	794–1185
Kamakura	1185–1333
Muromachi	1333–1574
Momoyama	1574–1603
Edo (Tokugawa)	1603–1867
Meiji	1868–1912
Taisho	1912–1926
Showa	1926–1989
Heisei	1989–

IMPORTANT ANNIVERSARIES
February 11, Commemoration of the founding
of the nation; May 3, Constitution Day;
December 23, Emperor Hirohito's birthday.

LEADERS IN LITERATURE
Osamu Dazai (writer)
Yasushi Inoue (writer)
Yasunari Kawabata (writer)
Yukio Mishima (writer)
Ogai Mori (writer)
Soseki Natsume (writer)
Naoya Shiga (writer)
Toson Shimazaki (poet and writer)
Junichiro Tanizaki (writer)

GLOSSARY

animism	Belief that all natural objects, such as trees and rocks, possess a soul.
daimyo	Feudal chieftain of old Japan.
haniwa	Clay sculpture, in the form of human/animal figures, buried with rich Japanese in ancient times.
kana	Japanese phonetic script.
matsuri	Festival.
miso	Rich, savory paste of malt, salt and fermented soy beans used in Japanese cooking.
odori	Dance.
sake	Japanese rice wine.
samurai	Japanese warrior of historical times.
Shogun	Military ruler of Japan.
seppuku	Ritual suicide by slitting the belly with a sword. The more common (vulgar) term is *harakiri*.
tofu	A soft or firm curd made from soy beans, a rich source of protein.
torii	Gateway to a Shinto shrine.

BIBLIOGRAPHY

Discover Japan (Volumes 1 & 2), Kodansha International,/USA Limited, New York, 1986.

Meyer, Carolyn: *A Voice from Japan—An Outsider Looks In*, Harcourt Brace Jovanovich, San Diego, 1988.

Wise, Michael, *Travellers' Tales of Old Japan*, Times Books International, Singapore 1987.

INDEX

Picture Credits

Sheila Brown, Jon Burbank, Jimmy Kang, Peter Korn, Harold Pfeiffer, Japanese Embassy of Singapore, Luca I. Tettoni

With special thanks to Mr. Futoshi Imanaka.